Professional Word Processing in Business and Legal Environments

Professional Word Processing in Business and Legal Environments

Mark W. Greenia

Reston Publishing Company, Inc.
A Prentice-Hall Company
Reston, Virginia

Library of Congress Cataloging in Publication Data

Greenia, Mark.
   Professional word processing in business and legal
environments.

   1. Word processing.   I. Title.
HF5548.115.G74   1985   652'.5   85-2022
ISBN 0-8359-5773-X

10   9   8   7   6   5   4   3   2   1

PRINTED IN THE UNITED STATES OF AMERICA

To Kathy
with Love

Contents

CHAPTER 1

CHAPTER 2

Acknowledgments

Although the ideas, opinions, and concepts expressed in this book are the responsibility of the author and do not necessarily represent the position of any of the groups listed below, grateful acknowledgment is extended to the following corporations and companies for their assistance by way of equipment photos, information or inspiration which helped towards the completion of this book:

Barrister Information Systems Corporation
Compuscan, Inc.
Dataproducts Corporation
Diablo Systems, Inc., a Xerox Company
General DataComm Industries, Inc.
Hewlett-Packard Company
Honeywell Information Systems, Inc.
International Business Machines Corporation
Lexitron Corporation/Telex Systems, Inc.
Multi-Tech Systems, Inc.
Qume Corporation, a subsidiary of ITT
Racal-Vadic Inc.
Syntrex, Inc.
Tab Products Company
Universal Data Systems Inc.
Viking Acoustical Corporation
Wang Laboratories, Inc.
Xerox Corporation

EPM™, 630 ECS™ are registered trademarks of Diablo Systems, Inc.,
a Xerox Company. Diablo and Xerox are registered trademarks of
Xerox Corporation. Sprint 11/40-130 PLUS™ is a registered trademark of Qume Corporation, a subsidiary of ITT. AlphaWord III+ is
a trademark of Compuscan®, Inc. LEXIS and NEXIS are trademarks
of Mead Data Central. OIS 40™ and OIS 50™ are trademarks of
Wang Laboratories, Inc.

Introduction

This book begins with a descriptive look at word processing technology, some of the different types of systems available, and the use of various peripheral devices with an eye towards clarifying some of the confusion that tends to surround a rapidly growing and somewhat complex field.

In Chapter 2 we take an overview of how word processing technology is applied to the general business environment. Various word processing career categories are described in detail along with a clarification of some key management terms. We look briefly at a sample organizational structure and a basic structure for small and large word processing departments. We cover some vital training tips for word processing instructors and trainees and the roles of marketing support representatives (MSRs) and professional consultants. This section also covers what to look for in a professional consultant and what they should be doing for you. Also discussed in this chapter are the importance of proper administration in getting word processing work done, the administrative tools necessary in order to turn out a professional product, and some useful guidelines to accomplish this.

In Chapter 3 we explore word processing as it relates to legal applications. The term *legal environment* includes both independent legal firms and legal offices or legal departments in a business or corporation. This chapter covers many areas of concern to the legal word processing specialist as well as legal management personnel. Covered are the advantages of word processing as it pertains to law practice, handling of legal fees and billings, points to keep in mind in processing legal documents, and various other related topics.

Chapter 4 covers choosing and setting up a word processing system and includes diagrams of some of the many system configurations possible.

Appendix A contains a listing of further reading and reference materials on various aspects of word and information processing. For easy reference, the subject areas are broken down into several categories.

Appendix B contains a listing of the addresses of major vendors for word processing and related equipment and services.

Appendix C is a detailed word and information processing glossary which the reader will find helpful in clarifying his/her understanding of the word/information processing terminology in use today.

As in most specialized fields, the word processing industry has developed its own terminology which, if undefined, can leave one confused or with the feeling of having missed something. This glossary was not compiled as an afterthought as in some technical booklets, nor does it define technical terms with vague or misleading definitions or highly technical descriptions that explain little.

Attempts have been made to present a clear description of each term listed. The glossary is therefore meant to be utilized as a working reference tool for individuals in operations, supervision, and management so that each understands the terms being used resulting in better understanding, communication, and a more productive working environment and facilitate training.

Appendix D is a brief glossary of some of the legal terms used in this book plus other key terms that the legal word processing specialist will undoubtedly come across in his/her work.

Appendix E gives listings of commonly used abbreviations in the fields of general business, legal, and information processing.

Businessmen, managers, or lawyers whose offices have not yet acquired a word processor or who are looking to expand their present system will also find this book helpful in providing an insight into the ever-expanding field of information processing applications.

In short, anyone involved in word processing will find something of interest and use in this book as well as new ideas and a new approach to the subject of professional word processing.

1 Word Processing—A Technical Review

It should be noted briefly that computers are grouped into three basic categories in terms of size and computing power. These are *microcomputers, minicomputers* and *mainframes*. Word processors and personal computers are all in the microcomputer category. Minicomputers are somewhat larger than micros and are used most often in business applications. Mainframes are quite large (such as the IBM 370) and are used where very large amounts of data are being processed at high speeds and when considerable accuracy is required.

The use of microcomputers has grown tremendously over the past five to ten years. Many small businesses that were formerly unable to afford the cost of a minicomputer or mainframe found that many of their information processing needs could be handled quite adequately with a good microcomputer, and at a far more attractive price.

Computer technology has evolved significantly over the years. Now, it can be said that there are five different generations of computers:

1

1. The first generation computers were the vacuum tube giants such as the ENIAC. These received the greatest use from 1946 to about 1958.

2. The second generation computers came with the development of transistors and roughly spanned the years from 1959 to 1964.

3. The third generation of computers was born with the development of solid state components in the early 1960s. Third generation computers are often characterized by their ability to support multiprogramming and multiprocessors as well as their overall capacity and performance. The IBM 360 and 370 series, the Honeywell 6000 series and the Control Data 6000 are some examples of third generation computers.

4. The fourth generation of computers saw the light of day with the advent of the computer chip and large scale integration (LSI) technologies, although with some systems it is difficult to draw an exact line between third and fourth generation technologies. The majority of computers in use today are third and fourth generation computers.

5. The "fifth generation" computer is still in the development stages to a large degree. This is the generation of "AI" or artificial intelligence.

Word processors and personal computers are considered mainly *fourth generation* computers and this is the type of computer we will be dealing with in this book.

THE DEVELOPMENT OF WORD PROCESSING

Electronic Typewriters

Electronic word processing as it is known today began in 1964 with the introduction of the IBM Magnetic Tape Selectric Typewriter (or MT/ST). The MT/ST utilized magnetic tape to electronically record the typist's keystrokes. By replaying the tape, the recorded material could be reprinted automatically. The MT/ST may be outmoded by today's standards, but at that time it offered typists and secretaries a very worthwhile savings in time and energy.

Video Display Terminals

In March 1970, a company called "AutoScribe" was formed. AutoScribe, which later became "Lexitron Corporation," developed and perfected the first word processing terminal which utilized a video display screen. These visual display screen terminals employed a cathode ray tube (CRT) which is similar in function to the picture tube in a television set. By using a video display screen, the typist could view an entire page of text and correct any errors in format, spelling, or typing before printing out the page. Video display screens offered a tremendous advantage to the world of office automation and signaled the first major change in office equipment and productivity since the introduction of the computer. By 1977, Lexitron Corporation had more visual display word processing terminals in use by more customers than any other equipment supplier. Today, there are more than 50 different suppliers of word processing equipment throughout the country. Some of the biggest names in the manufacturing of word processing equipment today include IBM, Wang, Xerox, NBI, Syntrex, CPT, Lanier, A.B. Dick, Digital Equipment Corporation, Barrister, and others.

WORD PROCESSING TODAY

Word processing can be broadly defined as the input, manipulation, storage, retrieval, and output of text. Since its modest beginnings in the early 1960's, word processing as a business and professional tool has grown from an innovative convenience into an administrative necessity. Many companies would find it extremely difficult if not impossible to maintain a competitive position in today's business world without the benefits of computerized word processing. Rapid advances in microprocessor technology coupled with an ever increasing demand for experienced word processing operators and competent supervisory personnel have sparked the growth of a whole new category of career professional—the *word processing specialist*. A word processing specialist is one who is skilled in the operation of electronic text editing equipment and capable of producing high quality, correctly formatted textual output in accordance with user requirements. The term "specialist" indicates that such an individual is not just a proficient operator, but has particular skills designed toward applications in a specific field. This includes such fields as accounting, legal, insurance, medical, news media, publishing, banking and many, many others. The are also various levels of specialization which we will look at more closely in Chapter 2.

WORD PROCESSING & DATA PROCESSING

Data processing and word processing both involve the processing of information. Data processing usually involves the handling of numerical information including statistics, accounting, financial summaries, payroll calculations, and any application which involves numerical data. Word processing, on the other hand, refers to the processing of text, e.g., letters, documents, articles, reports, etc. In some applications, the areas of word and data processing overlap. For example, a business may require automatic calculation and mailing of monthly billings statements each with a cover letter that is based on a standard format but individualized enough to bring the customer up to date on the status of his account. Such an application may call for equipment with both data processing and word processing capabilities. In the past few years, the term *information processing* has come into greater and greater use as a descriptive term covering both the data processing and word processing fields. Some businesses have integrated their word processing department with their data processing department, still calling it data processing or sometimes information processing. Others have not integrated word and data processing and maintain separate facilities, personnel, and organizational flow lines for each department. Some examples of how various departments and systems can be organized are discussed in Chapter 4. In the remainder of this chapter, we will take a look at the technical aspects of word processing, the different types of equipment available and some of the peripheral devices that are commonly used in the professional word processing environment.

WORD PROCESSING SYSTEMS

Personal Computers vs. Dedicated Systems

There are many types and configurations of word processors and word processing systems. Perhaps the best place to start is to describe the differences between word processing on a dedicated system and word processing done on a personal computer (PC). A "dedicated" word processor is basically a unit that is specifically designed, both in terms of hardware and software, for word processing applications. It is therefore "dedicated" to the task of word processing. The keyboard of a dedicated system is specially designed to make word processing fast, efficient, and easy. You may find that using a dedicated word processing system takes far fewer keystrokes to accomplish text editing than using many personal computers. With a dedicated system, the software is usually supplied by the manufacturer and the user does not need to concern himself with the software to any great degree, except to keep up to date with new options offered by the manufacturer and to update his software from time to time. A personal computer, on the other hand, is designed to perform a variety of functions and to run a large number of different types of software.

Word processing is only one of the many software packages available for personal computers.

Although a personal computer can perform many more functions than a dedicated word processing unit, when it comes to word processing alone the dedicated system is usually faster, more efficient, has greater reliability, and is more user friendly than a PC with a word processing software package. If word processing performance alone was the only point of decision, there would be little controversy over which to use. Overall cost of the system, however, plays a part as well. The price of personal computers has been dropping steadily over the past few years. A personal computer system (including video terminal, keyboard, printer, and software) can be purchased for considerably less than a dedicated word processing system. When making a choice as to which type of system to buy, ask yourself the following questions:

1. Will the word processing activity be needed on a full time basis, i.e., eight hours or more per day?
2. Is speed a factor in completing the word processing projects?
3. Will there be a large volume of word processing traffic?
4. Are the word processing requirements highly specialized, such as those needed for legal or accounting work?

If the answer to any of these questions is "yes," it is recommended that you look toward a dedicated word processing system to fill your needs. As traditional dedicated systems become more sophisticated in their computing abilities, and word processing software packages for personal computers become faster, easier, and more reliable, the gap between dedicated systems and the use of personal computers as word processors will continue to close. The dedicated system will not actually become extinct, but it will be forced to evolve into a more versatile type of business computing machine capable of playing a greatly expanded role in the fast-paced world of office automation. Word processing software for personal computers has been steadily improving over the past few years and even better programs can be expected in the near future.

If you decide to go with a personal computer, you will need to choose carefully the type of system you will get the most benefit from as well as become familiar with the different types of software available for word processing. The following is a sample listing of a some of the more well known programs along with the addresses of their suppliers. They are not listed in any particular order and no claims or endorsements are made here for any particular type of software.

"WordStar®"
MicroPro
1299 4th St.
San Rafael, CA 94901

"EasyWriter™"
Informational Unlimited
281 Arlington Ave.
Kennsington, CA 94707

"Volkswriter®"
Lifetree Software
411 Pacific
Monterey, CA 93940

"Scripsit™"
Radio Shack
P.O. Box 2910
Fort Worth, TX 76101

"Spellbinder™"
Lexisoft, Inc."
P.O. Box 267
Davis, CA 95616

"Select®"
Select Information Systems
919 Sir Francis Drake Blvd.
Kentfield, CA 94904

There are many good books available covering the use of a particular type of word processing software. It is recommended that potential users look over these carefully to get a feel of the capabilities and limitations of each of the various types. (See Appendix B for a listing of some of these books.) There are also many other very good word processing software packages not listed here. Check your local book store for computer books or magazines covering these. In addition, there are many magazines covering business software products which list the good and bad points in various current software packages. These are useful in getting an overview of what to look for and what to be wary of.

Operating Systems

Another aspect of software to take into account when you are using a personal computer as a word processor is the *operating system*. The operating system is a computer program or series of programs that controls the operation of the entire computer. The operating system supervises the input and output activities of the computer and is involved in assigning storage areas to information relating to other programs. The operating system for a particular type of equipment is usually supplied by the vendor. Some programs are designed to operate under a specific operating system, so it is wise to have some familiarity with the different types available. Some of the better known operating systems are listed below.

CP/M® CP/M stands for Control Program for Microcomputers. CP/M is an example of an operating system that handles one terminal. It acts as a standard software interface between user programs and system hardware. CP/M is a registered trademark of Digital Research Corporation. There are also updates and revisions of this operating system such as CP/M®80 and CP/M®86.

MP/P™ MP/P stands for multiprogamming control program for microprocessors. MP/P handles up to four different terminals while allowing those terminals to perform different tasks. MP/P™ is compatible with CP/M, meaning that programs created or formatted under a CP/M operating system will run under MP/P also. MP/P is also a registered trademark of Digital Research Corporation.

MS-DOS™ MS-DOS is an operating system developed by Microsoft Corporation which can be used with the 16 bit IBM personal computer. MS-DOS™ is a trademark of Microsoft Corporation.

PC-DOS PC-DOS is the IBM Personal Computer Disk Operating System.

UNIX™ UNIX is a trademark of AT&T Bell Laboratories.

XENIX™ XENIX is a multiuser, multitasking operating system developed by Microsoft. XENIX™ is a trademark of Microsoft Corporation.

New developments and improvements in software are being made every day. For a listing of further information sources concerning these and other software systems see Appendix A.

Another point to keep in mind when using a personal computer for word processing (WP) is that it may take slightly longer to train personnel in the use of word processing software on a personal computer (PC) than it may take on a dedicated system. One reason is that with a WP software package, a PC often requires the use of control keys and

Using a Personal Computer for Word Processing

function keys in order to carry out the editing procedures. It may take a little while to become familiar with the use of such keys, but once familiarity is established, they can be made to function adequately. One may also find some reluctance on the part of secretarial or WP personnel who have worked for years on a dedicated system and who are now being asked to leave that and learn to operate a PC with WP software. Such reluctance is usually temporary, but should not be completely unexpected when making a major transition of this type. As a last point, many lower priced personal computers/micro computers do not come equipped with the heavy duty, high speed, high quality printers that one usually finds as part of a dedicated system. This can be a factor if one is expecting heavy work loads with a corresponding demand for high quality. This situation, too, may be changing in the near future.

Standalone Systems

A standalone system is a complete word processing unit consisting of microprocessor, keyboard, screen, disk drives, printer, and software that is capable of operating fully without support from any outside processing unit (see Figures 1-1, 1-2, and 1-3). A standalone system has several advantages. It is usually fairly compact and fits comfortably into the modern office structure. It can be operated full time by a secretary or word processing operator without drawing CPU time or storage space from any other office systems. Since it is independent, it is not affected by downtime or system failures of any other office computers. It can be moved and relocated without too much difficulty.

Figure 1-1. IBM Displaywriter™ with full page screen display is an example of a standalone word processor. *(Photo courtesy of IBM Corporation.)*

Figure 1-2. Syntrex Aquarius™ multifunction workstation (background) can be equipped to interface with the IBM® PC (foreground). *(Photo courtesy of Syntrex, Inc.)*

Figure 1-3. The Xerox® 820-II personal computer is both a standalone system and an entry level professional workstation on the company's Ethernet office communications network. *(Photo courtesy of Xerox Corporation.)*

Multi-Terminal Systems

A multi-terminal system (see Figures 1-4 and 1-5) is a system employing more than one word processing terminal in a specific interconnected arrangement. There are two main types of multi-terminal systems. These are *shared logic* systems and *shared resource* systems.

Shared Logic System

In a shared logic system, the terminal workstations utilize a common central processing unit. The terminals themselves may be "dumb" terminals, i.e., terminals having no independent logic capabilities and only able to function when connected to the main CPU, or they may be "intelligent" terminals that can be used both as standalone processors and as dumb terminals for the main CPU.

Figure 1-6 illustrates a shared logic system where each of four dumb terminals utilizes a common central processing unit and hard disk storage facility. In this example, each station has its own printer.

Figure 1-4. The Honeywell MicroSystem 6/10™ professional business system is a modular, single-station microcomputer with extensive office processing capabilities.
(Photo courtesy of Honeywell Inc.)

Figure 1-5. The Wang OIS 40® and OIS 50®
offer advanced word/information processing in
standalone and small cluster environments.
(Photo courtesy of Wang Laboratories, Inc.)

Shared Resource System

In a shared resource system, the terminal workstations share one or more common peripheral devices, such as a high speed printer, optical character reader, or other device.

Figure 1-7 is a shared resource system and shows four smart terminals sharing a single laser printer. The terminals also share a single letter quality printer for each two terminals in the system. This method of sharing some of the more expensive pieces of equipment makes it possible to keep costs down while still providing numerous operators with access to vital equipment. Many variations of such arrangements are possible.

Local Area Networks

A local area network (LAN) is an interconnection of word processing terminals that can communicate with one another and share one or more peripheral devices such as a central storage facility, optical character readers, or printers, or can share a central processing unit. There can be many different configurations of local area networks. Some LANs utilize standalone word processors which are online to share a central storage bank, e.g., a hard disk. LANs can help keep

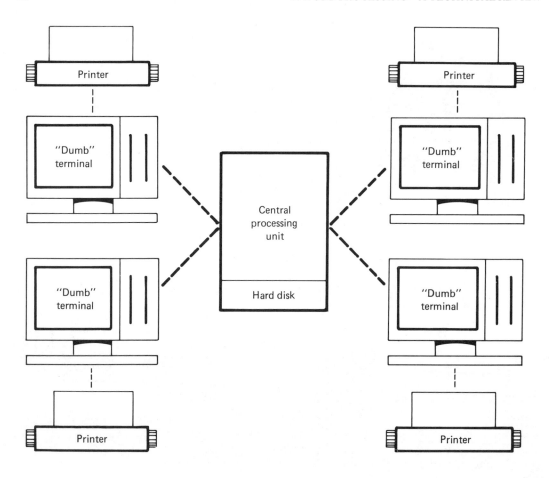

Figure 1-6.   A Shared Logic System

down equipment costs by sharing the more expensive equipment with more than one word processing terminal. Such networking can also be used to send and receive intraoffice electronic mail.

Figure 1-8 illustrates a simple local area network consisting of four operator terminals, two shared letter quality printers and a shared laser printer. All the terminals in this network are capable of communicatng with one another.

Micro-Mainframe
Links

Perhaps one of the more interesting uses of local area networks in business is the interfacing of word processing terminals and/or personal computers with the large central data banks and central proc-

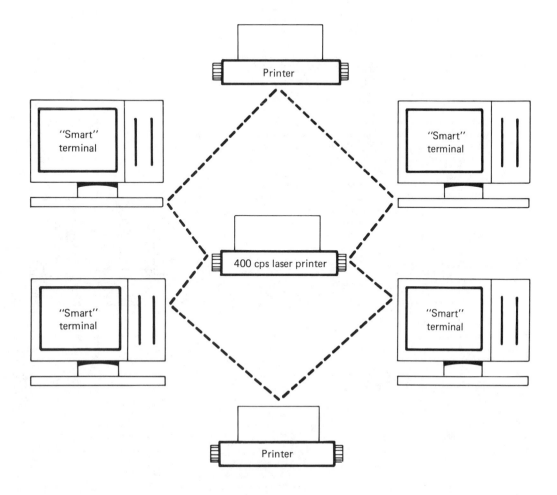

Figure 1-7. A Shared Resource System

essing unit of a large (mainframe) computer system. By so doing, businesses can utilize the power and capacity of the mainframe along with the versatility of the personal computer or word processor. Such applications go beyond traditional word processing alone and may be designed for use by managers interested in data base utilization, and as a powerful, online management aide. This "marriage" of the micro to the mainframe will likely be seen in more and more applications as managers seek to utilize the power of existing computer resources that their companies already have along with the conveniences and necessities of having their own personal workstations. Figure 1-9 shows an example of the micro-mainframe marriage.

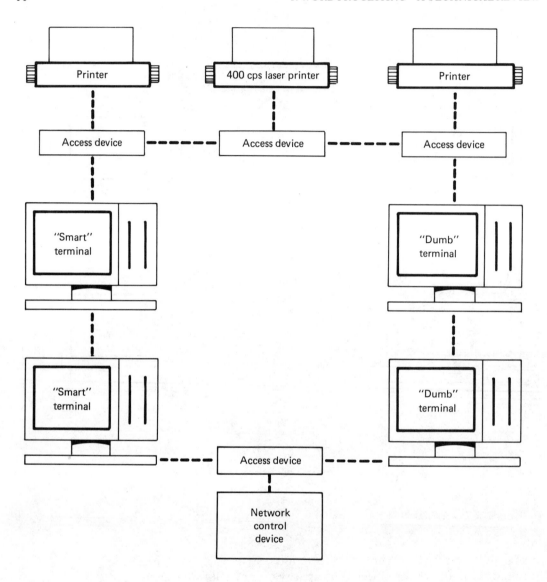

Figure 1-8. Simple Local Area Network

MEMORY & STORAGE

To understand the difference between memory and storage it may be convenient to think of *memory* as "live" information within the WP terminal and *storage* as "inactive" information waiting to be accessed and used. Live information is represented in the microprocessor circuitry as a series of "on" or "off" values or switches. An electronic switch can

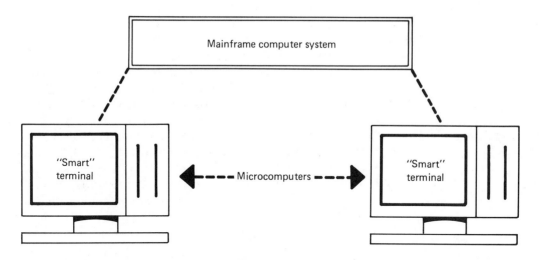

Figure 1-9. Mainframe Computer System. *Possible Utilizations*: word processing, data input, data retrieval, accounting, data base access, graphics, calendaring, intraoffice communication, and electronic mail.

be "on" (represented by the binary value "1") or "off" (represented by the binary value "0"). This live information is referred to as "volatile," i.e., it is subject to accidental loss or distortion through:

complete electrical power loss

electrical power surge or reduction

machine malfunction

operator error (e.g., accidental deletion).

In most diskette based WP systems, this type of information loss or distortion is not uncommon, however, the quantity of information involved usually is not large since the live memory capacity of most WP systems is fairly limited. Retrieving data from memory is much faster than retrieving data from storage. However, since memory is made up of complex electronic circuitry, it is much more expensive per unit of area than is storage. Consequently, the live memory capacity of most personal computers/word processors is relatively small. A PC/WP usually has anywhere from 16 to 256K bytes of memory space available. Since live memory must hold the operating system program, the software currently being run, and the data being processed, main memory alone is insufficient to hold all the needed data for effective word processing or personal computing. Therefore, external storage facilities are needed. One of the least expensive methods of external storage and one of the most common is the floppy disk. A floppy disk is a flexible, flat, circular-shaped disk which is capable of random access storage of information. They are called floppy because they are flexible in comparison to hard disks. Floppy disks come in various sizes. Most common is the mini-floppy (5-¼×5-¼). Floppies also come in the standard 8 inch and also the micro-floppy (3 to 3-½ inch) diskette. Some floppies are designed to store information on only one side. Others are capable of storing information on both sides. The amount of data stored per unit of area of the floppy disk is referred to as "density." A dual density disk is capable of storing roughly twice the amount of information as a single density disk.

Figure 1-10 shows a 5-¼ inch floppy disk or "diskette" such as those used in many word processing and personal computer systems.

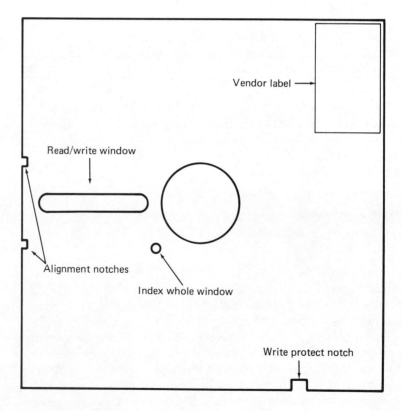

Figure 1-10. 5-¼ inch floppy diskette

Some manufacturers use specially formatted diskettes for their equipment and such diskettes may *not* be compatible with other equipment. Inserting a diskette into a WP/PC terminal which is not designed to accept that diskette's particular format characteristics may result in damage to the diskette and a consequent loss of data. Check to see what types of diskettes are compatible with your equipment before experimenting.

Diskettes are subject to damage and therefore loss of valuable information if not handled with care. Here are some important suggestions in the care of diskettes.

CARE OF DISKETTES

1. Never touch the surface of the diskette itself, either through the read/write window or around the center hole.

2. Do not bend the diskette or rest it flat with heavy objects on top of it.

3. Keep the diskette in its protective paper jacket when not in use.

4. Use only a felt tip pen to write on the label of a diskette jacket and even then do not press down too heavily. It is preferable to write only on the outer protective paper jacket.

5. Do not allow the surface of a diskette to be scratched.

6. Do not attach clamps or paper clips to diskettes or hold them together with rubber bands.

7. Keep diskettes free of moisture and dirt.

8. Keep diskettes away from magnets or strong magnetic fields as this may cause loss of stored information.

9. Keep the diskettes free from extremes of heat or cold. Storage temperatures should not be allowed to drop below 60°F or exceed 110°F.

10. Insert the diskette into the computer/word processor drive carefully. Never jam or force diskettes into place.

11. Last, but not least, keep your diskettes in a safe place. Program diskettes and information (working) diskettes can be expensive to replace, not to mention the cost of time and resources that could be involved in attempting to reconstruct any lost information. Diskettes can be stored overnight in locked, fireproof cabinets specially built for this purpose.

The relative storage capacity of various storage media can be seen in Table 1-1.

Storage Capacity

TABLE 1-1. Storage Capacities

Disk Size	Sides	Density	Capacity	Characters	Pages
Micro-floppy	1	single	286K	200,000	100
Micro-floppy	2	single	572K	400,000	200
Mini-floppy	1	single	150K	120,000	60
Mini-floppy	2	single	300K	160,000	80
Mini-floppy	1	dual	300K	160,000	80
Mini-floppy	2	dual	600K	320,000	160
Floppy (8″)	1	single	300K	240,000	120
Floppy (8″)	1	dual	600K	480,000	240
Floppy (8″)	2	dual	1200K	960,000	480
Hard Disks			1M	800,000	400
Hard Disks			2.5M	2,000,000	1,000
Hard Disks			5M	4,000,000	2,000
Hard Disks			10M	8,000,000	4,000
Hard Disks			15M	12,000,000	6,000
Hard Disks			16M	12,800,000	6,400
Hard Disks			20M	16,000,000	8,000
Hard Disks			30M	24,000,000	12,000
Hard Disks			60M	48,000,000	24,000
Hard Disks			120M	96,000,000	48,000

(The above scale gives an approximation only and is based on an average of 2,000 characters per page.)

Note:

1 byte	= 8 bits (*bi*nary digi*ts*) = one character of data
1 K (or 1Kb)	= 1 kilobyte = 1024 bytes (8,192 bits)
1 M (or 1 Mb)	= 1 megabyte = 1,048,576 bytes (8,388,608 bits)

When ordering or using floppy disks, it is important to note which format you are looking for. Some machines will take only one particular type. Here are a few abbreviations one might see and what they stand for.

page

ss/sd	single sided, single density	6 0
ss/dd	single sided, double density	8 0
ds/sd	double sided, single density	8 0
ds/dd	double sided, double density	1 6 0
r	reversible (a diskette that can be inserted one way and then taken out and flipped around top to bottom and inserted the other way. Also sometimes called a "flippy.")

PRINTERS

There are two broad categories of technology when it comes to word processing printers. These are *impact* printers and *non-impact* printers. Impact printers rely on a striking mechanism and some sort of ink/carbon ribbon in order to make a character impression on the surface of the paper. Non-impact printers use other methods of producing characters such as heat (thermal printers) or charged particles (electrostatic printers). In choosing a printer, the main considerations are *quality*, *speed*, and *cost*.

Quality

Printing quality is extremely important in business and legal applications. The highest quality printers are those that produce the clearest character resolution and have excellent legibility and uniformity. As this type of printer is most often used for professional and business letters, it has come to be known in the word processing field as "letter quality." Higher speed printers usually sacrifice such high quality for greater output volume. These printers are most often used for rapid production of vast amounts of data, or for reports and other documents where quality of the type is not of primary importance. This lesser grade of resolution quality is sometimes referred to as "draft quality."

Speed

Printing speed is measured most often in "cps" which stands for characters per second. Very high speed printers often have output speeds measured in lines per minute (lpm). To give some idea of the speeds represented by these measurements, an average letter quality printer for a home computer will have a printing speed anywhere from 15 to 35 cps. A high quality daisywheel printer used for word processing in a business office might operate at speeds ranging from 45 to 55 cps. A higher speed, draft quality printer, such as dot matrix, may have a speed of 200 cps or more. Large chain printers, which are less commonly used for wp applications, can achieve speeds of 500 to 1000 lpm or more. And the technology doesn't stop there. The top-of-the-line laser printers can reach speeds of over 24 pages per minute! For a comparison of indicated printing speeds and actual output time, see Table 1-2.

Cost

Just as with WP terminals, printer costs vary with the quality of the equipment and the state of the technology. A good quality, 25 cps

TABLE 1-2. Comparison of Printing Speeds
and Output Times

Printer Speed	WPM	LPN	Output Time For One Typed Page
30 cps	360	36	1.4 minutes
35 cps	420	42	1.2 minutes
40 cps	480	48	1.04 minutes
55 cps	660	66	50 seconds
120 cps	1440	144	35 seconds
200 cps	2400	240	12 seconds
400 cps	4800	480	6 seconds

daisywheel printer for home computer use will range from $300 to $1,200. A high quality, 55 cps daisywheel printer for professional office use will usually run about $800 to $3,000. Standard dot matrix printers range from $900 to $3,500; other printers, such as chain printers, run much higher. The cost of laser printers has been in the tens of thousands until just recently. The new Hewlett-Packard LazerJet® Printer, for example, can turn out letter quality text at a rate of about eight pages per minute at a cost of around $3,500. Some laser printers reach output speeds of 24 pages per minute or more. These laser printers hover in the ten to sixty thousand dollar range.

(The prices here are estimates for comparison only. The prices on printers have been steadily dropping over recent years due to improvements in technology and increasing demand.)

Types of Printing

Typeball. The typeball printing element is similar in size to a golf ball and has raised characters in a series of rings around its surface. The typeball is mounted on an axis which causes it to rotate, tilt, and impact against the paper when the desired character is in position.

Daisywheel. The daisywheel printer uses a plastic or metal typing element shaped like a daisy. The characters are located on the outer edge of the "petals" of the daisy element which is rotated into position at high speed. The "petals" are struck with a hammer-like mechanism to transfer the ink onto the paper.

Thimble. The thimble printer is very similar to a daisywheel, but its printing element is shaped more like a thimble. The petals of the thimble element each have two raised characters. The thimble is rotated into the proper position for printing a specific character and then impacted by a hammer device which transfers the character imprint to the paper through a ribbon.

Dot Matrix. A dot matrix printer uses a series of pins or hammers that strike out from a block and hit the paper in various positions in order to form characters. The output from such matrix printers can usually be seen to be made up of tiny dots. Although dot matrix printers are often quite fast, the quality of output is usually not as good as daisywheel or thimble type printers. The quality of a dot matrix printer depends to some extent on the density of the dots used to make up each character. Some dot matrix printers have variable density which results in variable speed and output quality.

Infinite Dot Matrix. Infinite dot matrix is a high density dot matrix, i.e., a special procedure used to make the dots overlap and give the appearance of a whole character. Infinite dot matrix printers are capable of much higher quality resolution and rival the quality produced by daisywheel printers. Such matrix printers are capable of very good graphics resolution.

Chain Printer. A chain printer utilizes a high speed chain with raised characters moving past a series of impacting hammers.

Band Printer. A band printer utilizes a rotating band with raised characters. As the character moves into the correct position for printing, one of a series of hammers impacts the paper and ribbon against the band leaving the character impression on the paper.

Laser Printer. One method of laser printing uses a laser light source focused on a spinning mirror and reflected across the surface of a printing drum which has a high positive electrical charge. The areas of the drum struck by the laser become negatively charged and attract positively charged particles of the toner (ink). This is then output onto paper as hard copy. Laser printers also use dot matrix character formation, but the matrix is extremely fine, e.g., approximately 300 dots per inch, which produces type of letter quality resolution.

Ink Jet Printer. An ink jet printer produces dot matrix type characters by shooting electrostatically charged ink drops against the surface of the paper.

Thermal Printer. A thermal printer is a non-impact printer which uses a heating element to produce an image on the paper. Some thermal printers will only operate using special heat-sensitive paper while others will work fine using ordinary white paper.

Table 1-3 shows a comparison of the different kinds of printers.

Compatibility

Compatibility refers to the ability of different computer/word processing devices to interface with each other and operate successfully without the need for hardware or software modification. It is important to note that not all systems will be compatible with the same print-

TABLE 1-3. Relative Speed and Quality Comparisons

Name	Type	Average Maximum Speeds	Average Output Quality
TYPEBALL	IMPACT	16 cps	EXCELLENT
DAISYWHEEL	IMPACT	55 cps	EXCELLENT
THIMBLE	IMPACT	55 cps	EXCELLENT
STANDARD DOT MATRIX	IMPACT	600 cps	FAIR—GOOD
INFINITE DOT MATRIX	IMPACT	200 cps	VERY GOOD
CHAIN PRINTER	IMPACT	500 lpm[+]	FAIR—GOOD
BAND PRINTER	IMPACT	500 lpm[+]	FAIR—GOOD
BELT PRINTER	IMPACT	500 lpm[+]	FAIR—GOOD
LASER PRINTER	NON-IMPACT	20 pgs/min[+]	EXCELLENT
INK-JET PRINTER	NON-IMPACT	200 cps[+]	VERY GOOD
THERMAL PRINTER	NON-IMPACT	200 cps[+]	VERY GOOD

In comparing the manufacturer listed printing speed of printers, remember that with longer documents it takes a certain amount of time for automatic paper feed devices to position the paper into place for each page. Some auto feed devices are faster than others and this should be taken into account when you are looking into a new printer since it may be advisable to observe a full demonstration and figure out for yourself the actual time it will take the printer to complete a lengthy document.

ers without some special handling. For example, many personal computers are designed to output to printers in the *serial* transmission mode, while many dedicated word processing systems are designed to output to printers using *parallel* transmission. The difference between serial and parallel transmission is the manner in which the data is transferred. Parallel transmission means that all eight bits of a signal are transmitted at the same time on separate paths. Parallel data transmission is a bit more sophisticated than serial transmission, but it is also much faster. Needless to say, you cannot connect a parallel connector to a serial port or vice versa. Even if you could, the two systems are not directly compatible so it is important to check this point when you plan to connect various peripheral units to your PC or WP. You may, of course, find some systems that are capable of handling both serial and parallel data transmission.

Figures 1-11 to 1-14 show a few of the many different printers available on the market.

OCR : OPTICAL CHARACTER READERS

Optical Character Reader. An OCR is a device capable of scanning pages of typed or printed text and converting that data into electronic signals for input to a computer or word processing terminal.

Figure 1-11. The Diablo EPM2™ Electronic Printing Machine is an example of a thermal printer which uses a unique heat transfer system resulting in high quality text output. The EPM2 can turn out typed pages at the rate of six pages per minute. *(Photo courtesy of Diablo Systems, Inc., a Xerox Company.)*

Figure 1-12. The Diablo 630 ECS™ 40 cps letter quality printer. *(Photo courtesy of Diablo Systems, Inc., a Xerox Company.)*

Figure 1-13.   The SPRINT 11/40-130 PLUS™ by
Qume Corporation is available in 15 inch width or
widetrack format. *(Photo courtesy of Qume Corporation,
a subsidiary of ITT.)*

Optical Character Recognition. The identification of graphic characters by the use of a photosensitive scanning device.

Despite the speed at which word processing systems can manipulate text, process revisions, automatically reformat, and perform numerous other complex functions, a great deal of time can be consumed in manually inputting original data or text into a word processing system. To avoid the unwise use of expensive word processing terminals solely as original input devices, many offices have invested in an Optical Character Reader. (See Figures 1-15 and 1-16.) With an OCR device, typists and secretarial staff can be utilized to type handwritten material which can then be fed into an OCR for rapid input directly into the word processing system without having to be retyped on the word processing terminals. Depending on the quality and capability of the OCR device, documents may be typed using one or more acceptable type fonts. Some OCR devices will only read a special OCR style font which requires that any typewriters to be used for typing OCR input material be properly equipped with the proper OCR typing element. Many higher quality OCR devices have the capability of reading many different types of fonts including

Figure 1-14. The Hewlett-Packard LazerJet®
printer is a high-speed, letter quality printer
capable of output speeds of eight pages per minute
(approximately 7-½ seconds per page). The
LazerJet printer is also capable of mixing up to
four different type styles on a single page and has
virtually noiseless operation.
(Photos courtesy of Hewlett-Packard.)

Figure 1-15. Compuscan's AlphaWord® Series 80
PageReader. *(Photo courtesy of Compuscan, Inc.)*

Figure 1-16. Compuscan's AlphaWord III+
Optical Character Reader. *(Photo courtesy of
Compuscan, Inc.)*

standard types such as "Courier 10." One advantage of such higher quality OCRs is, of course, that data already typed does not have to be retyped using an OCR element. Another advantage is that such higher quality OCR's usually have better reading capabilities as well.

(Although OCR equipment may differ in exactly how it scans and processes text, the following steps cover the basic procedure followed by such systems.)

How OCRs Work

1. The OCR is connected to a word processor/computer terminal that has communications capability. This is usually done "direct-wired" using a communications interfacing cable and RS-232 connectors, but can be done over phone lines using modems at each end of the line.
2. A page is fed into position to be read by the scanner.
3. The OCR device scans each page line by line.
4. The character information on the page is converted into digital information and interpreted by the recognition logic which "recognizes" each character scanned. This is sometimes done by comparison with stored character representations within the logic of the OCR.
5. Non-recognized characters are "flagged" by the system; i.e., a special character, such as an "*" or "@" sign, is logically inserted next to the questionable character.
6. The digital information is output to a word processing/computer terminal which records it onto its storage medium (diskette, hard disk, etc.).
7. Steps 2 to 6 are repeated until the whole document has been scanned in this fashion.

The word processing operator proceeds to "clean up" the text now on the word processor, usually by doing a global search for the flagged characters and comparing the text visually to the typewritten original. The error rate in a good OCR reader is about one misread per six page of text.

Processing of OCR Input Text

The OCR photoscanning sensors are often adjusted to be insensitive to red felt pen. The typist/secretary can indicate in red any typos/changes on the typed copy and these red markings will be ignored by the OCR. The word processing operator can later make the indicated changes once the information has been input into the WP terminal.

It is important that the original copy be clean and free from smudges, stray pen/pencil marks, and other imperfections. The sensitive scanning mechanism may be thrown off by these markings and cause extraneous characters to be added to the text, or they may cause the scanner to be thrown off and therefore misread entire pages. Good OCRs can usually read photocopies of typed text as well. Excess photocopy ink should be watched for and corrected if possible to avoid confusing the scanner. Also, the typing elements of the typewriters used to type original text for input should be in a good condition. Clear, distinct characters produce the best results for OCR. Worn ribbons and broken or worn elements can cause the number of misreads to increase, some of which can even escape the flagging mechanisms of the OCR. A broken or indistinct "8" may be read as a "3" for example, or zeros may be misread as the letter O or vice versa. These points should be watched for in order to avoid headaches and costly mistakes. Different OCR devices have different capabilities and the operations manual for your OCR should be carefully reviewed and followed to get the most benefit from your machine.

Cost Outlay

OCRs cost anywhere from $5,000 to $30,000 and in some cases run as high as $100,000.

Cost Savings

In offices where a great deal of straight input of text is needed, an OCR can save valuable time as well as the expense of acquiring additional WP terminals for manual input.

Additional Uses for an OCR

An OCR device can be useful in other ways as well. For example:

1. Hard copy can be produced by a word processor in one location and sent over long distances by mail or courier and then be input via OCR into another WP terminal at a second location. This might be useful for areas that do not have telecommunications equipment. There is also less risk of damage to hard copy in transit then there might be to magnetic storage media such as floppy disks.

2. OCRs can be used in some cases as a link between two word processing systems that are not compatible. Documents can be printed out by one system and input via OCR into the other system without the need for special conversion equipment. Although not optimum for large amounts of document processing, it is a valid emergency method to overcome machine incompatibility on small projects.

3. Law firms, for example, can use OCR equipment to input certain portions of documents filed by an opposing party, such as interrogatory questions, and can then insert their answers to each specific question without having to re-input each question. The final output would be a sequential listing of questions and responses formatted as a single document, which flows logically and which is often more convenient for attorneys on both sides as well as for the court.

ELECTRONIC MAIL

Electronic mail is the sending and receiving of documents over interconnecting cables or telephone lines using word processing/computer terminals. Electronic mail is many times faster than other types of document transfer such as photofaxing or standard courier methods. Whole documents can be transferred between two separate locations in seconds as long as each is equipped with a word processor/ computer terminal with communications capability and a modem— and of course a phone line. With the proper type of modem, called an auto-answer modem, it is not even required that there be a person operating the terminal at the receiving end. The person at the receiving end can put his terminal in the receive mode, modem on auto-answer, and then leave. Whenever the sender is ready, he/she simply dials the phone number of the receiving office and when the connection is made, transmits. Through the auto-answer modem, the receiving terminal automatically receives and stores the information sent.

Since modems come in various types and have different options available, one should be aware of which functions will be needed to fill office communication demands. Let's take a closer look at the different kinds of modems and their capabilities.

MODEMS

A *modem* is a device used to transmit or receive data over telephone lines. Internally, computers and word processors operate on digital signals. In order for information to be passed electronically from one computer or device to another over conventional phone lines, the *digital* signals of the computer must be converted into audio or *analog* signals. A modem is used to convert the digital signals of a computer or word processor into analog signals which can be carried over phone lines. At the receiving point, the analog signals are then converted back into digital signals and fed to the other computer or wp terminal. The process of converting digital signals into analog signals is called *modulation*. The reverse, converting analog signals into digital signals, is called *demodulation*. The word *modem* is actually an acronym for the words *modulator-demodulator*. Figure 1-17 shows how a modem operates.

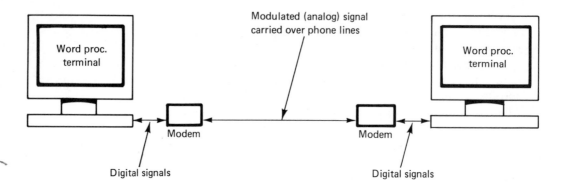

Figure 1-17.   How a Modem Operates

Modem Types and Capabilities

The following information provides a better understanding of the various types and capabilities of the modems available.

1. Types.
   a. Accoustic Coupled—signals are passed through the headset of a telephone rather than direct wired.
   b. Direct Connected—signals are passed over a direct line from modem to telephone jack.
2. Operation Modes.
   a. Simplex—transmits only in one direction.
   b. Half-duplex—transmits in both directions but not simultaneously.
   c. Full-duplex—simultaneous transmission in both directions.
3. Transmission Mode.
   a. Synchronous—characters of data are transmitted at a fixed rate with transmitter and receiver synchronized.
   b. Asynchronous—data is sent at varying intervals rather than at a fixed rate.
4. Receive/Send Capabilities.
   a. Originate—(Simplex).
   b. Answer—(Simplex).
   c. Originate & Answer—(Half-duplex or Full-duplex).
5. Additional Capabilities.
   a. Auto-dial—modem is capable of dialing a preset phone number and establishing a connection with the receiving modem

without the operator having to dial the number by hand each time he wants to transmit information.

b. Auto-answer—modem answers incoming calls automatically and does not require a WP operator be present at all times on the receiving end.

Indicators

Most modems are equipped with a series of indicators which light up to give the operator information as to the status of various aspects of terminal readiness and other factors. (See Figures 1-18, 1-19, and 1-20) Since some manufacturers may have their own special indicators, the following list is not meant to be all inclusive. It does, however, provide descriptions of many of the indicators that one will see on modems. For a complete listing of the indicators, you will need to consult the modem operations manual for your particular brand of equipment.

DTE   Data Terminal Equipment (WP terminal, OCR, computer, etc.)
DCE   Data Communication Equipment (modem)
DS   Data Set (modem)
DTR   Data Terminal Ready—indicator that data terminal is ready
DSR   Data Set Ready—indicator that data set or modem is ready
RTS   Request To Send
DCD   Data Carrier Detect
CD   Carrier Detect
CXR   Carrier Signal Received
RLSD   Received Line Signal Detector
CTS   Clear To Send
RI   Ring Indicator

VDT SAFEGUARDS

It comes as no big surprise that operators who sit in front of video display terminals all day long are exposed to a certain amount of radiation. There has been much discussion in recent years about the possible dangers of such radiation. A complete analysis of the long or short term effects of such radiation and its possible hazards are beyond the scope of this book. However, to minimize exposure time and ease working strain, the following suggestions for word processing operators may be helpful.

1. Take short breaks between long work projects. Get up and walk away from the screen for a few minutes.

Figure 1-18.   Racal-Vadic VA 3451 Modem. *(Photo courtesy of Racal-Vadic.)*

2. Take regular breaks during the day—at least ten minutes every two hours or so.

3. When you are on break, eating lunch, or working on other aspects of production such as proofreading, etc., move away from the terminal screen, or if practical, turn it off.

Figure 1-19.   Racal-Vadic Auto Dial VA 212 Modem. *(Photo courtesy of Racal-Vadic.)*

Figure 1-20.   Universal Data Systems Modem.
(Photo courtesy of Universal Data Systems.)

4. When the work day is done, engage in some extroverting activity,
    i.e., don't just go home and plop down in front of the TV set (an-
    other source of CRT radiation). Take a walk, look around, or go
    jogging perhaps.

5. If you have persistent eye problems, headaches or other ailments,
    don't ignore them. Get a medical and/or eye exam, and don't neg-
    lect to mention to your doctor that you operate a VDT.

Controversy still exists in this area and research into possible
VDT dangers is continuing. Operators should keep aware of the information being made available on this subject. As more data becomes
available, we will hopefully see the information processing industry,
particularly the equipment manufacturers, take a more active role in
the development of better safeguards for video terminal operators if
such safeguards are proven necessary. With the continued growth of
word processing as a profession, word processing associations and organizations are receiving greater respect and are becoming a more active and influential voice in calling for better research into this area
and for better safeguards for terminal users.

VDT News, a bi-monthly newsletter published by Louis Slesin, offers specific information concerning VDT operator health and safety, as well as data on technical research and office automation. For subscription information, write to:

VDT News
P.O. Box 1799
Grand Central Station
New York, N.Y. 10163

2 The Business Environment

The term "business" is a broad term covering a large variety of transactions, most of which have in common various aspects of production, marketing, financing, and the exchanging of goods or provision of services. Among the vast number of businesses today which have benefitted from the advances in word processing technology are:

law firms
accounting firms
banks
publishing companies
brokerage firms
real estate
advertising agencies
oil companies
insurance companies
communications companies
hospitals
newspapers
airlines
book stores

TYPES OF USERS

libraries

auto rentals

mail order houses

small businesses

employment agencies

Almost every major business endeavor has been touched in some way or fashion by the word processing boom. Also, one of the biggest users of word processing technology is, of course, government, at federal, state, and local levels, including agencies of all types and public service companies. Along with this introduction of high tech word processing into the business environment came a need for a reorganization of the traditional office environment. Trained word processing operators placed in key positions caused production output to double or triple. Production flow lines needed to be revised in many cases to accommodate this new production source, and organizational structures in many cases had to be revised to include positions such as Word Processing Supervisor, Information Processing Manager, Administrative Support Specialist, and other similar positions and titles. Competition became stiffer and the need to expand office automation activities became more acute.

In addition, with this expansion came, as it often does, a little confusion. More and more word/information products hit the market; new vendors sprang up; and a new terminology was spawned which has continued to grow. Some business enterprises slid into this new era of word processing automation with remarkable ease and efficiency, seeing in it higher productivity, higher quality results, and ultimately higher profits. Others found it a more difficult adjustment and others still are trying to find their feet. The expansion of technology has, however, refused to slow down and wait for anyone to catch their breath.

Over the past ten years, word processing job positions have become more specialized. For persons who have a word processing department or unit within their sphere of responsibility, it is wise to know that these different positions exist. The very nature of the word processing environment will cause these different positions to evolve into being even in organizations where they are not specifically labeled. In running a large word processing operation, knowledge of these various positions is vital.

Here follows a description of various professional word processing positions and the levels of skill and experience associated with each.

WORD PROCESSING TRAINEE

Experience: Entry Level: 0—12 months
Skills: Adequate typing, grammar, spelling, punctuation, formatting, transcription, document creation, text editing, and wp machine skills.

WORD PROCESSING OPERATOR

Experience: 1—2 years
Skills: Excellent typing, grammar, spelling, punctuation, formatting, transcription, document creation, text editing, OCR, and wp machine skills.

WORD PROCESSING SPECIALIST

Experience: Over 2 years
Skills: All skills listed above plus specialized knowledge in a particular area such as legal, accounting, insurance, etc., and experience with various types of wp support equipment such as telecommunications devices.

WORD PROCESSING SENIOR SPECIALIST/ ASSISTANT SUPERVISOR

Experience: 2 — 3 years
Skills: All skills listed above plus the ability to adequately supervise others. May be in charge of a department or a section of a department. Good interpersonal communication skills.

WORD PROCESSING SUPERVISOR/SENIOR SUPERVISOR

Experience: 4 — 5 years
Skills: All above skills. Coordinates department activities, reports directly to word processing manager. May be in charge of all phases of personnel procurement for his/her department. Overall responsibility for production of department, training of new personnel, layout and adequacy of word processing system. Makes any needed recommendations to management regarding improvements or upgrades in equipment or working conditions.

WORD PROCESSING MANAGER/INFORMATION PROCESSING MANAGER

Experience: Five years, including managerial experience, a working knowledge of various word processing system configurations, and usually familiarity with one or more computer languages.

Skills: All above skills, but usually not involved with direct operation of equipment. May supervise both word processing and data processing activities where these are separate facilities. Reports directly to management. Responsible for overall production. Makes any needed recommendations to management regarding improvements or upgrades in systems or organizational lines.

ADDITIONAL WORD PROCESSING RELATED POSITIONS

WORD PROCESSING SECRETARY

Experience: Both experience as a secretary and in operating word processing equipment.

Skills: Good secretarial skills including excellent typing and transcription. Depending on working environment may also need shorthand ability, legal knowledge, and other administrative abilities.

WORD PROCESSING INSTRUCTOR

Experience: Over 2 years

Skills: Above average word processing skills, including an ability to work with and train others. Preferably has a working knowledge of a large number of systems. Keeps up to date on new developments in word processing industry.

WORD PROCESSING CONSULTANT

Experience: Usually 5 or more years with specialized knowledge in a particular application or applications. Ideally, would have first hand experience in all phases of information processing from operations to management, as well as good knowledge of systems and office organization. Keeps up to date on new developments in word processing and has personal contacts within various vendor companies, but is not tied to or working on behalf of any one vendor or commissioned to promote any one product. Able to spot the cause of production problems and recommend adequate handlings in terms of improved office automation.

THE MEANING OF ORGANIZATION/LEVELS OF MANAGEMENT

Organization. An organization is a group of individuals having specific responsibilities who are united for a common purpose or work. An organization is composed of trained individuals who are in communication with one another and who follow certain guidelines in order to produce a given product or achieve a specified goal.

Organization

There are three basic levels of organization: *Management, supervision,* and *operations.* Although businesses may differ in how their internal structures are set up, and differ as to what terminology is used for various echelons or departments, these three basic levels will be found in some form in all business enterprises. In the very small business, one person can hold positions in all three of these levels simultaneously. In large businesses, the divisions between these three levels are more easily seen. It is important for those in business to recognize the primary activities and functions of each of the levels of organization in order to achieve a high level of agreement and communication within an organization. Here follows a brief description and definition of each of these levels.

Management. Management consists of the alignment of the activities of an organization toward the attainment of the goals and purposes of that organization.

Management

There can be various subdivisions of management. For our purposes here, the two key divisions are *administrative management* and *intermediate management.*

Administrative Management. Administrative management is the level at which the goals and purposes of the organization are defined and policy is established. Sometimes referred to as Top Management.

Intermediate Management. Intermediate management is the level at which the policy and plans of administrative management are communicated broadly to supervisory personnel for implementation.

Management's primary activities and areas of concern include:

observation

evaluation

planning

coordination

policy development

organization

guidance

execution

major approvals

financial solvency

organizational viability

cost accountancy

overall production

personnel procurement

personnel training

personnel utilization

equipment utilization

communications

public relations

marketing

expansion

Supervision

Supervision. Supervision is the coordination point between *management* and *operations*. A supervisor is responsible for the day-to-day production and viability of the areas within his/her immediate sphere of authority. Supervision is the level just below *intermediate management* and is sometimes referred to as *operations management*.

A supervisor is concerned with monitoring production flow lines, removing barriers that may inhibit production, and ensuring that personnel know how to do their jobs, that production is kept in a viable range, and that staff morale is high. It is worthy of note that in areas where production is low, morale will often be found to be low also. Bringing about an increase in production will usually bring about an increase in morale as well. Where supervisory authority is abused, however, and staff are mishandled, both production and morale will drop.

Supervision's primary activities and areas of concern include:

overall workload

priorities

reports to management concerning production related activities staff schedules

production quality

availability of supplies

equipment performance

staff morale

user requirements

hiring of staff

staff training & enhancement

new technical developments

communication difficulties

conflicting demands

Operations. Operations is involved in actual front-line production. Operations staff would be those with specific skills or duties who are involved in a specific phase of production.

Operations

Operation's primary activities and areas of concern include:

user requirements

priorities

production deadlines

formats

technical proficiency

product quality

equipment operation

equipment upgrades

The above definitions do not exclude the fact that operations staff do have certain supervisory responsibilities and supervisory personnel do have some management duties. Each individual, whether in operations, supervision, or management, has to be able to control and handle those activities within his/her immediate area. It is the size of the area of responsibility that determines the level of management skill required. For example, an individual may be highly proficient at operating a word processor and capable of turning out high quality, high volume work, but in order to be successful in a supervisory position, he must be able to expand his sphere of control so that it encompasses a whole department or unit. As one moves higher and higher up the organizational ladder, communication skills become more and more important. A manager who can't communicate easily and effectively with his superiors, juniors, and co-managers, is to that degree out of touch with the organization as a whole. Only to the degree that he is able to employ effective communication skills will he be able to forward the goals and purposes of the organization and maintain the necessary personal interaction with his co-workers. Figure 2-1 shows a basic organization chart and Figure 2-2 provides examples of small and large office organization.

PRODUCTION FLOW LINES

Efficiency. Effective operation as measured by the quality and quantity of production in comparison with the expenditure of money and resources and the utilization of time and personnel.

The key to efficiency is the ability to manage. Management of resources, personnel, time, and production flow lines is vital to obtain volume production on a viable basis. Poor or absent management results in wasted effort, lost money, and inadequate or no products. A production flow line is a channel along which particles of one kind or another flow, stop, change, and start again with the end result a finished product. There may be numerous individuals along any one production flow line. Efficient management of the work particles along such a line is the responsibility of not only the production supervisor or manager, but of each individual stationed along that line. Efficient management consists of adequate control over the working environment. Control of the working environment includes control over equipment, supplies, communication lines, and actions. Where production flow lines are well established and maintained, and individuals are trained in the actions necessary to produce the desired products, quality production can be brought about and maintained by efficient management.

Efficiency Checklist

To increase production, supervisors and managers need to look for things that by their presence or absence inhibit production. Some of these factors include:

1. *Lack of personnel:* i.e., a vacant position on the production flow line.
2. *Untrained personnel:* personnel who do not know what they are supposed to do or how to do it.
3. *Unnamed products:* a vague demand for production without having named the exact products desired.
4. *Incorrectly named products:* demands for products that should be produced by some other department or activity, or demands for products that are not actually needed by anyone.

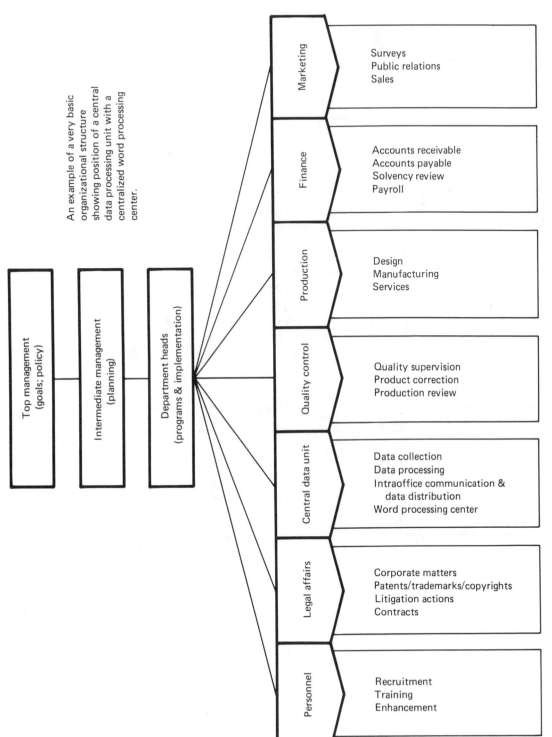

An example of a very basic organizational structure showing position of a central data processing unit with a centralized word processing center.

Top management
(goals; policy)

Intermediate management
(planning)

Department heads
(programs & implementation)

Marketing
Surveys
Public relations
Sales

Finance
Accounts receivable
Accounts payable
Solvency review
Payroll

Production
Design
Manufacturing
Services

Quality control
Quality supervision
Product correction
Production review

Central data unit
Data collection
Data processing
Intraoffice communication &
  data distribution
Word processing center

Legal affairs
Corporate matters
Patents/trademarks/copyrights
Litigation actions
Contracts

Personnel
Recruitment
Training
Enhancement

Figure 2-1.   Basic Organization Chart

Small office structure with three WP operators:

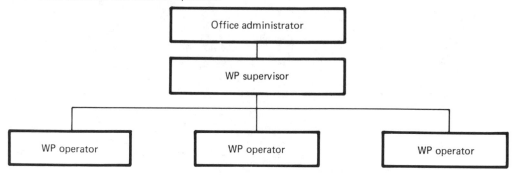

Larger office structure with centralized word processing center and 14 (or more) operators.

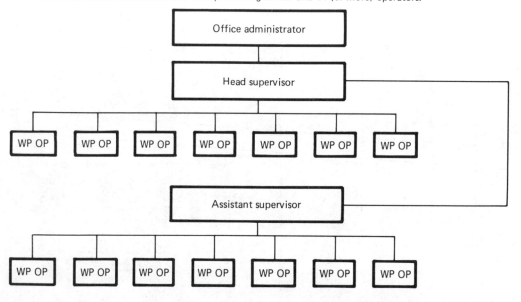

Figure 2-2. Organization Chart for Word
Processing Departments

5. *Cross-ordered products:* demands to produce one product as opposed to counter demands to produce something else. Conflicting
   demands reflect a confusion of basic organizational lines and put
   a strain on personnel while wasting valuable production time.

6. *Arbitrary instructions:* arbitrary instructions to take actions or make
   changes contrary to initial instructions or to accepted standards
   which result in a product that does not fill the desired need.

7. *Lack of materials:* absence of raw materials and supplies needed to produce the products.

8. *Unknown lines:* personnel on the production flow line who may not realize they are on a line or even that production lines exist, thus causing confusion.

9. *Invalidation of personnel:* harsh treatment of personnel, unreal demands, and orders which cannot realistically be fulfilled; threats of termination or reprimand all serve to inhibit quality production although they seemingly produce an increase in activity.

10. *Inadequate technical equipment:* technical equipment which is outdated or inadequate for current production demands.

11. *Insufficient technical equipment:* the technology of existing equipment may be adequate, but there is not enough of such equipment available to meet demands.

This checklist should be completed by a first-hand inspection of the working environment carried out by either the supervisor of the area or the office administrator. More than one point on the checklist may need correction, and some may require more handling than others.

THE IMPORTANCE OF ADMINISTRATION

Correct administration is vital to the operation of a word processing department, no matter how small. The larger the flow of traffic into and out of the word processing center, the greater the role correct administration will play. By administration we mean the process of getting one's work successfully completed and returned to the correct user as rapidly and efficiently as possible. *Administration* comes from the Latin *ministrare* meaning *to serve.* A word processing center or even a single word processing operator is providing a valuable service to another person or to a large number of people. The term *administration* encompasses all the functions and procedures required for optimum production.

Administrative Tools for Word Processing Operators

General Information

The professional word processing operator requires an assortment of administrative tools in order to perform his/her job successfully. These may include the following information:

1. Name, address, and phone number of vendors for *each* type of equipment in use. This may require separate numbers for:

equipment installation

equipment maintenance and repair

sales information/MSR

technical queries

2. Name, address, and phone numbers of reliable temporary agencies and freelance temporaries who know how to use your equipment and can be available on short notice for emergencies.

3. List of other office personnel you will be dealing with, their job title, department name, and intraoffice phone number.

4. Manual of general office policies (working hours, breaks, vacations, insurance benefits, etc.).

5. Manual of in-house formats and procedures with samples of letters and other documents, etc.

Specialized Reference Manuals and Publications

1. Equipment operation manuals (supplied by vendor/manufacturer) for each piece of equipment.

2. In-house documentation and memos concerning various aspects of equipment operation, supplemental to information supplied by vendors.

3. English dictionaries.

4. Grammar and punctuation reference guides.

5. Secretarial handbooks.

6. Directories for zip codes and other address information.

7. Word/information processing dictionaries and handbooks.

8. Supply catalogs, information letters on new developments, and any useful vendor publications.

9. Specialized resources and guides for a particular area of work such as accounting, legal, insurance, medical, etc.

Basic Supplies

blank diskettes, tapes, or other storage media

typing ribbons

extra printwheels or typing elements

letterhead paper

envelopes (all needed sizes)

paper (all needed sizes)

carbon paper

paper clips

stapler

pens/pencils

rulers

correction fluid

paper tape

routing slips

WP instruction forms

Getting the Work Done Correctly

Getting the word processing work done correctly depends to a large degree on getting the exact instructions communicated from the user to the WP operator. The worst way to do this is to neglect to do it at all and to assume the WP operators know by mental telepathy what it is the user is requesting. The second worst way is to give the WP operator brief verbal instructions only. This can lead to misinterpretation, omission of key details by the user, or confusion for the operator who probably has five or ten other projects waiting in line for his/her attention as well. The best way to avoid problems is to **put all instructions in writing.** Most larger WP centers have developed their own handy printed forms for this. These forms can be custom designed for any type of business activity and can be either long and detailed or short and simple as the work demands. Having the instructions in writing protects both the operator and the user and leads to better relations and better, more professional service all around.

A sample WORD PROCESSING INSTRUCTION FORM is shown in Figure 2-3. Figure 2-4 shows the same form after it has been completed. Figure 2-5 shows an example of proper editing style.

PROOF-READING GUIDELINES

Proofreading is a skill unto itself. Whether you are a word processing specialist, secretary, typist or professional proofreader, there are certain guidelines which may be very helpful in achieving a high degree of accuracy in proofreading. Here are some of the more useful guidelines.

1. When proofreading, do just that. Don't listen to music, eat a snack, or do something else while attempting to proofread at the same time. Give it your *full* attention. Don't rush it.

2. Make sure you are in a comfortable position with sufficient light, and have the height of your chair and table adjusted comfortably.

WORD PROCESSING INSTRUCTION FORM

TO: WORD PROCESSING   TODAY'S DATE: _____

FROM: _____   QUERIES
                                        CONTACT: _____
RETURN TO: _____
            ━━━━━━━━━━━━━━   Phone: _____

TITLE OF DOCUMENT: _____

PRIORITY: A   IMMEDIATE TURN-AROUND REQUESTED
                 REASON:
(Circle one)   _____

             B   NEEDED BY _____ O'CLOCK TODAY
                 REASON:

                 _____

             C   NORMAL TRAFFIC (8 hour turn around)

             D   LOW PRIORITY; NEEDED BY _____

HANDLING INSTRUCTIONS

/__/   INPUT ONLY (OCR MATERIAL)

/__/   MAKE INDICATED REVISIONS, PRINT ANOTHER DRAFT

/__/   MAKE INDICATED REVISIONS, PRINT IN FINAL FORM

/__/   OTHER _____

       _____

FORMAT   PAPER

/__/   SINGLE SPACING   /__/   WHITE BOND

/__/   DOUBLE SPACING   /__/   PLAIN WHITE

/__/   OTHER _____   /__/   OFFICE LETTERHEAD

                                /__/   OTHER _____

COPIES NEEDED: /__/   8-1/2 x 11 inch

_____   /__/   8-1/2 x 14 inch

                                /__/   OTHER _____

Figure 2-3. A Sample Word Processing
Instruction Form

48

WORD PROCESSING INSTRUCTION FORM

TO: WORD PROCESSING   TODAY'S DATE: _9/11/86_

FROM: _J. B._   QUERIES

RETURN TO: _J. B._   CONTACT: _JACK_

                            Phone: _814_

TITLE OF DOCUMENT: _LETTER TO MR. SIMS_

PRIORITY: (A)   IMMEDIATE TURN-AROUND REQUESTED

(Circle one)   REASON: _AM GOING OUT OF TOWN_

           B   NEEDED BY _____ O'CLOCK TODAY
               REASON:
               _____

           C   NORMAL TRAFFIC (8 hour turn around)

           D   LOW PRIORITY; NEEDED BY _____

HANDLING INSTRUCTIONS

/ /   INPUT ONLY (OCR MATERIAL)

/ /   MAKE INDICATED REVISIONS, PRINT ANOTHER DRAFT

/X/   MAKE INDICATED REVISIONS, PRINT IN FINAL FORM

/ /   OTHER _____

               _____

FORMAT	PAPER
/X/ SINGLE SPACING	/ / WHITE BOND
/ / DOUBLE SPACING	/ / PLAIN WHITE
/ / OTHER _____	/X/ OFFICE LETTERHEAD
	/ / OTHER _____
COPIES NEEDED:	/ / 8-1/2 x 11 inch
_3_	/ / 8-1/2 x 14 inch
	/ / OTHER _____

Figure 2-4. A Completed Word Processing
Instruction Form

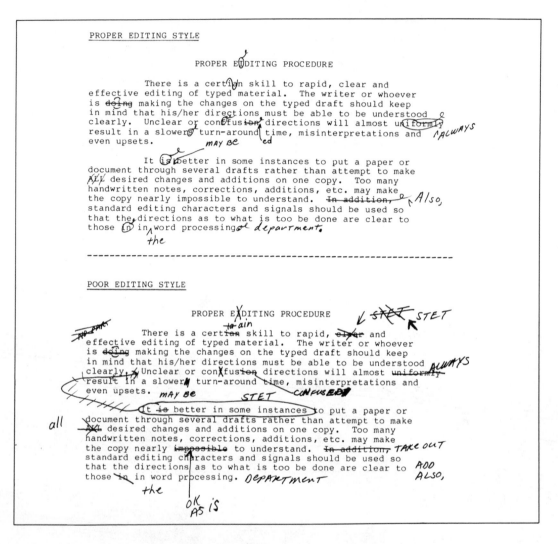

Figure 2-5. Proper Editing Style

3. Minimize distractions such as office noise, interruptions, or other distractions.

4. Check first the overall format, e.g., paper size, paper color, margins, titles, headings, subheadings, date, etc.

5. Check for errors by category, such as typing errors, printer errors (broken or missing characters), spelling, grammar, punctuation, and content.

6. Read the text backwards from right to left, looking at each word individually rather than as a string of words to check for spelling errors. Once this has been done, however, it is important to go back and read the text normally, this time proofing it for content.

7. Check to see that any additions, deletions, etc. as indicated on the edited copy have been made correctly if you are proofreading a document which has been revised according to an edited copy.

8. Check columns of numbers on documents that have been read into word processing via OCR for possible misreads, such as 8's being mistaken for 3's and zeros being mistaken for the letter O, and any others that may be peculiar to your particular type of equipment.

9. Have adequate reference manuals at your disposal such as dictionaries, grammar books, and other needed materials and be familiar with them so you can quickly spot and correct errors in any of the categories mentioned above.

Following these simple tips may help you to boost your proofreading ability to high, professional standards.

An important piece of administration for larger word processing centers is a Word Processing Production Log. Such a log is useful to monitor the traffic load of projects coming into the WP center and also to keep track of who the work is being done for—which may be of interest to companies that charge their clients specially for word processing work done on the client's behalf.

Figure 2-6 is a sample log. Many variations are possible.

Logging Work Projects and Production Time

Figures 2-7 through 2-12 show sample formats for various business-related documents and forms. The exact formats for these will depend on the specific application for which they are used, but those shown here are representative of many of the types commonly used.

Examples of Business Formats

WORD PROCESSING TRAINING TIPS

A word processing instructor is one who trains others in the use of word processing equipment and other skills required to be a proficient word processing operator. Instructors may be in-house em-

Word Processing Instructors

WORD PROCESSING PRODUCTION LOG   NAME: *MARY SMITH*

DEPT.: *WORD PROC.*

DATE	DOC. TITLE	ORIG.INPUT/REVISIONS	TIME HRS.	DISK. REF.	USER I.D.
8/2	MEMO TO V.P	REVISIONS	.50	LK5	MJK
8/2	BILLS SUMMARY	FINAL COPY	1.00	B52	DLJ
8/3	LTR TO SMITH	REVISIONS	.25	CL8	CL

Figure 2-6. Sample Log

ployees, teachers at professional schools, or freelance word processing trainers.

Training

Training consists of two complementary phases:

1. Theory.
2. Hands-on experience.

Neither phase by itself will produce the same results in the same amount of time as can be achieved by a balanced approach consisting of both theory and hands-on experience. They can be done as separate courses, i.e., a theory course first then hands on, or they can be done almost simultaneously. Optimumly, the word processing trainee should have the equipment available in front of him/her when studying the theory. This way the information becomes more readily related to the actual components to be used and the student will be better in touch with the subject as a whole. Employing this approach, the instructor will also be able to more rapidly spot questions and confusions that the student may have in using the equipment he is being trained on. There is no substitute for having a trained instructor pres-

```
          L E X I K O N   S E R V I C E S

          WORD PROCESSING SPECIALISTS
          _____


WORD PROCESSING                              LEGAL
TRAINING                                     FINANCIAL
CONSULTANCY                                  EDUCATIONAL


January 23, 1986


Personnel Manager
Techno-Chemical Products Corporation
3458 Grayline Avenue
Los Angeles, CA  90024


Dear Sir:

Our service is pleased to make available to your organization
the highest quality secretarial and word processing services
possible on a consistant and reliable basis.  You will find
our staff are experts in various types of office automation
equipment and various levels of office administration.  If
you need additional word processing or clerical support
staff of any kind, please contact me at the number listed
on the enclosed booklet.  The booklet describes in further
detail the services available from Lexikon.

Looking forward to assisting you in your office automation
needs.

Very truly yours,



Michael Gregory
Personnel Assignment Officer


MFG:rl
[MFG3]


Encl.
```

Figure 2-7. Sample Business Letter

CONSOLIDATED DATA SERVICES, INC.

Data Processing Specialists

M E M O R A N D U M

TO: T. K. Sims

FROM: J. J. Hildebrandt   DATE: 9/24/86

CC: Comptroller Files   FILE NO.:   01714

       Re: Mainframe Equipment Leasing Corp.,
            Tech-City, Massachusetts

The contract for leasing our IBM System 370 computer equipment
expires at the end of next month. Please ensure that a new
lease is signed extending our operation rights another 3 years.
Please see to it as well that the new service contract is reviewed
by our in-house attorneys and approved by them before we
commit ourselves to any long-term financial obligations.

Your rapid handling of this is essential since our guaranteed
renewal option is due to expire in less than 60 days.

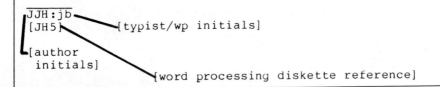

JJH:jb
[JH5]   [typist/wp initials]

[author
 initials]
                     [word processing diskette reference]

Figure 2-8. Sample Business Memorandum

ent to walk-through the basic procedures in operating word processing equipment with the trainee. Theory alone will usually only ex-
pose a fraction of the questions which the student may encounter.
Also, this simultaneous approach most closely duplicates the working
environment where the word processing operator will have his/her
terminal along with operations and procedure manuals to go by.

```
┌─────────────────────────────────────────────────────────────────┐
│                                                                   │
│            SEVEN-DWARFS MINING COMPANY, INC.                      │
│                                                                   │
│          M I N U T E S   O F   M E E T I N G                      │
│                                                                   │
│  TO:                                                              │
│                                                                   │
│  All Staff                              October 5, 1987           │
│                                                                   │
│                                                                   │
│                                                                   │
│  Attending:  Happy          Absent:  Bashful                      │
│              Dopey                    Sleepy                       │
│              Grumpy                                                │
│              Sneezy                                               │
│              Doc                                                  │
│                                                                   │
│                                                                   │
│  WORK SCHEDULE -- It was voted unanimously by those present       │
│  to modify the daytime work schedule from 6:00 a.m. to 3:00 p.m., │
│  to 7:00 a.m. to 4:00 p.m.                                        │
│                                                                   │
│                                                                   │
│  TOOLS PURCHASING -- The expected shipment of new mining tools    │
│  which had been delayed by lack of funds is now due to arrive     │
│  C.O.D. early next week.  Sufficient funds are available in       │
│  the treasury office.                                             │
│                                                                   │
│                                                                   │
│  INSURANCE --  Insurance coverage has been changed from United    │
│  Insurance Exchange Co. to a new company -- Miners Insurance Co., │
│  Inc. of Albany, New York.                                        │
│                                                                   │
│                                                                   │
│  PRODUCTION QUOTAS -- Production quotas are being met and exceeded │
│  regularly.                                                       │
│                                                                   │
│                                                                   │
│  NEXT MEETING --  The meeting was adjourned after 30 minutes.  The │
│  next meeting is scheduled for November 5, 1987.                  │
│                                                                   │
│                                                                   │
│                                                                   │
│                                   _____     │
│  _____                                S. B. White               │
│  SBW:sl                            Meeting Secretary             │
│                                                                   │
└─────────────────────────────────────────────────────────────────┘
```

Figure 2-9. Sample Minutes of Meeting

```
                    HIGH-TECH ENGINEERING CORPORATION

                    M E M O R A N D U M


    TO:     Accounts Dept.                    Date:    4/6/86

    FROM:   Payroll Dept.


    Re:   Salary Update


    Employee Name            Employee Number           Salary

    Lester H. Wilkins          23455-9885           $ 35,000.00

    Paul J. Samuels            34578-8933           $ 45,000.00

    Mary L. Smith              34567-1234           $ 34,000.00

    William T. Resdin          34556-7655           $ 34,500.00

    Frances R. Edwards         45678-3423           $ 34,500.00

    Matthew W. Green           34545-7878           $ 22,500.00

    Robert K. Michell          39394-4838           $ 56,500.00

    David L. Williams          30293-2872           $ 25,500.00



    TLH:rt
```

Figure 2-10. Sample Business Memo "High-Tech
Engineering Corporation"

Theory   The theory consists of basic word processing terminology and
                    definitions, word processing concepts, a brief description of different
                    types of terminals, and detailed instructions as to the operation of a
                    particular type of equipment. Charts, diagrams, and photographs are
                    very helpful in theory training.

```
                    HIGH-TECH ENGINEERING CORPORATION
              _____


                  JOB PERFORMANCE EVALUATION FORM


        DEPARTMENT:          _____  DATES: _____ to _____

        EMPLOYEE NAME:       _____

        POSITION TITLE:      _____

        SUPERVISOR NAME:     _____

        PERSON DOING THIS
          EVALUATION:        _____


        CATEGORY                       PERFORMANCE RATING


        OVERALL JOB PERFORMANCE     POOR   GOOD   V.GOOD   EXCELLENT

        SKILL IMPROVEMENT           POOR   GOOD   V.GOOD   EXCELLENT

        TECHNICAL PROFICIENCY       POOR   GOOD   V.GOOD   EXCELLENT

        ABILITY TO MEET ASSIGNED    POOR   GOOD   V.GOOD   EXCELLENT
          DEADLINES

        PERFORMANCE UNDER PRESSURE  POOR   GOOD   V.GOOD   EXCELLENT

        PARTICIPATION IN
          GROUP WORK PROJECTS       POOR   GOOD   V.GOOD   EXCELLENT

        INTERACTION WITH OTHER
          EMPLOYEES                 POOR   GOOD   V.GOOD   EXCELLENT

        RELATIONSHIP WITH
          SUPERVISORY PERSONNEL     POOR   GOOD   V.GOOD   EXCELLENT


        COMMENTS: _____

        _____


        RECOMMENDATIONS: _____

        _____


        SIGNATURE: _____  DATE: _____
```

Figure 2-11. Job Performance Evaluation Form

```
MARY SMITH
4567 East Long St. Suite 44
Los Angeles, California 90078
(213) 345-9190
```

OBJECTIVE   WORD PROCESSING SUPERVISOR in a stimulating
                   environment offering growth potential and a
                   creative outlet for my skills and abilities.

QUALIFICATIONS   BS in Business Administration, supervisory and
                   management experience, 8 years word processing
                   experience

WORD PROCESSING
SKILLS   Proficient in operating many different word
                   processing systems including WANG OIS 40,
                   LANIER NO-PROBLEM, IBM DISPLAYWRITER,
                   LEXITRON VT1303, SYNTREX and others,

OTHER SKILLS   Experienced with telecommunications, PC
                   color-graphics, WP software for IBM PC,
                   Optical Character Readers

EDUCATION   BS in Business Administration
                   Illinois University
                   Chicago, Illnois,   graduated 6/1969

                   DIPLOMA in Word Processing Systems
                   Transwestern Institute of Information Processing
                   Los Angeles, California,   graduated 8/1983

EMPLOYMENT   WORD PROCESSING SPECIALIST   5 years
                   United Insurance Company
                   Brenton Way
                   Albany, New York
                       Responsible for revisions and proofreading
                       of insurance documents, business letters, etc.

                   WORD PROCESSING SUPERVISOR   3 years
                   LEE & McKENNA
                   ATTORNEYS AT LAW
                   New York, New York
                       Responsible for supervision of word
                       processing department of 10 staff,
                       purchasing of equipment, liason with
                       management and data processing personnel
                       and all phases of production

PERSONAL   Willing to relocate if needed. Non-smoker.

REFERENCES   Available on request.

Figure 2-12. Sample Résumé

Hands-on experience consists of working on the terminal directly, with an equipment manual available, under the supervision of a trained instructor. Small work assignments can be given to the student to familiarize him/her with the basic functions of the machine and to help indicate to the instructor where additional help may be needed.

Hands-on Experience

Part of hands-on experience should include working with various types of business formats such as legal, medical, insurance and others in order to become familiar with operating a word processing system in different business applications.

The two phases of theory and hands-on experience can be used to increase ability and proficiency. For example, once the student has gone through the basic theory and hands-on work once, he can then be exposed to more advanced theory followed by more advanced work assignments, then to specialized theory followed by specialized work assignments, and so on until the student is brought up to a high level of competency. It is recommended that a student be taught the basic operation of one type of word processing equipment to the point where he/she can operate it confidently before switching to other types of equipment. Switching the student from one type of machine to another too rapidly can cause a loss of confidence and can slow down overall training completion time. Students should also be trained on equipment types that they will actually be using in the working environment, rather than older, out of date equipment. Training should match as closely as possible the actual work environment that the student will be experiencing.

Spiral Approach

In addition to equipment training, there are two types of skills that an instructor should be aware of. These are foundation skills and specialization skills.

Foundation skills are those that undercut the technology of operating any one type of equipment. Foundation skills would include a knowledge of basic grammar, spelling, punctuation, and the use of the language itself. The ability to type accurately and to do basic tape transcription would fall under foundation skills.

Foundation Skills

Specialization skills are those that go beyond the basic skills needed to operate WP equipment. Specialization skills include a knowledge of business letter formats, various legal document formats, and other specialized formats for whatever area of specialization the operator is involved in. Specialization skills could also include telecom-

Specialization Skills

munications, computer programming, familiarity with systems analysis, data base, color graphics and other skills related to the information processing field. There is almost no limit to the scope of specialization skills. The trainee should be exposed to a variety of such applications but not be expected to study such skills extensively during his/her initial training period. Continued practice will bring about a high level of competence in the basic operations skills and from there the door will be open for the experienced word processor to advance into higher levels of skills and new areas of specialization.

Length of Training

For the experienced secretary/typist, a training course to become familiar with the basic operation skills of a word processor can take anywhere from 5 to 15 days. Of course, such training for a person with little or no typing/secretarial experience will take longer. Some schools offer professional word processing training programs that last from 1 to 8 weeks or more depending on the depth to which the subject is covered, and whether one is learning to operate one type of word processor only or several different types.

Cost of Training

Cost varies greatly. Courses can range from $75 to $1500 depending on the nature of the curriculum. It is best to have a basic idea of what one wants to learn and then shop around for the school that fits one's needs. Some schools will teach typing, basic grammar, spelling, business letter formats, and other administrative skills in addition to word processing training. Other schools concentrate on teaching operation of the equipment. Some vendors offer free training on their equipment when it is purchased or leased. This may involve sending staff to seminars or training sessions, or having a representative from the vendor come to the place of business and train the staff on the premises.

In-House Training

In businesses which employ large numbers of word processing personnel and where staff turnover is likely to be high, it is optimum to have at least a basic in-house training program where new personnel are grooved into the system and long term personnel are encouraged to advance and improve their abilities.

A supervisor or assistant supervisor can often double as a word processing instructor. He/she should be a proficient operator in his/her own right, be able to communicate well with other people, and be familiar with the points of training as described above.

Never underestimate the value of training. In many cases it is good policy to invest in the training of your own office or company staff since they already have the day-to-day working experience within your office environment to which they can relate new technical or administrative information. Such staff become much more valuable to the company and should be awarded with increased compensation so as not to lose them to other businesses or firms.

    Adequate staff training not only brings about increased productivity for the business office, it brings about a feeling of accomplishment and greater self respect for the those who receive such training. Proper training of supervisory and operations staff can also be an exercise in cost efficiency. High-tech equipment, whether microcomputer or dedicated word processor, is far more likely to pay for itself when operated and supervised by individuals who fully understand its functions and capabilities and who feel confident in their own ability to utilize the equipment to its fullest capabilities.

The Value of Training

The marketing support representative (MSR) is a link between the equipment vendor and the customer. The MSR stays in close communication with the customer to ensure the equipment is functioning properly and sees that any queries regarding equipment operation are handled. This often requires a number of visits to the customer's place of business to see the equipment and individuals in their day-to-day working environment and show them first hand how to operate any new equipment or implement a new type of software. Afterwards, when things are running smoothly, the MSR still keeps in communication by telephone and/or letter to stay in touch with those using the equipment directly. The duties of the MSR include assisting in any needed training of personnel on new systems or procedures, keeping the customer up to date on new developments in hardware or software that may relate to a specific customer's applications, and maintaining an open communication line with the customer to handle any problems or requests that may arise. A good MSR is a very valuable asset to both the customer and the vendor. Many problems or potential problems can be rapidly resolved through quick and competent handling by an MSR. It is usually of added benefit to be able to deal with the same MSR over a long period of time, since the MSR will have become familiar with the customer's business operations, the products involved, and the types of demands and difficulties that are likely to arise. Having a stable MSR who is in good communication also means that he/she will know what system or organizational

MARKETING SUPPORT REPRESEN- TATIVES (MSR)

changes have been made by the user company in the past and which suggestions have proven successful and which have not. With such a foundation of experience and insight into the needs of the customer, the MSR is much more able to provide the customer with a helpful and valuable service.

If you are not getting satisfaction from your MSR and are unable to get matters resolved easily, it is suggested that you make the situation known to the senior representatives of the vendor company and request that a different MSR be assigned to your account. Like any professional service provided to your business, you have a right to expect the best treatment possible since your equipment investment and staff productivity are so very closely affected.

Technical Support

In some cases there will arise technical questions that are beyond the scope of the MSR's training and expertise. When this happens, it is best to have a reliable member of the vendor's technical support staff to turn to for technical questions and advice. The technical support staff will usually know the equipment better than any of your operators or supervisors and should be very willing and able to help sort out any technical bugs that may arise or to assist in interfacing the vendor's brand of equipment with other types of equipments. In times of business office expansion where new and different types of equipment and peripherals are being set up to communicate with one another, assistance and advice from competent technical support personnel is invaluable and can save lots of time and money as well as headaches.

THE ROLE OF A CONSUL-TANT

A consultant is a hired professional whose job it is to provide insight into the nature of the operational and expansion problems facing a business activity and to provide solutions to those problems. A consultant is essentially a professional problem solver. To do this efficiently, a consultant must have the freedom to think in terms of various different equipment configurations and system concepts and not be tied to any one vendor's product line. Objectivity is a key factor in the decision making capability of the consultant. The consultant, if he is worth his fee, must also be able to speak his mind and call the shots as he sees them; not rely on telling the customer only what he wants to hear. If the consultant feels that the customer's expansion plans are unrealistic or poorly planned, he should say so. That is what he is being paid for. He should also say **why** the plans are inadequate and provide alternate **solutions.**

1. *Competence.* If you are using a consultant in the information processing area, he should have some first hand experience with the subject. He should have a working knowledge of several word processing systems as well as a good grasp of state-of-the-art advancements in the field. He should be highly conversant with the terminology used, but not try to befuddle others with the use of technical terms alone. He should have experience with organizational structures and various types of working environments. Above all he should know that he is a hired problem solver and should be both creative and realistic in his solutions.

2. *Communication Skills.* A consultant needs to have a very high ability to communicate, which means not only getting his point across, but more importantly, listening to others. The consultant will be communicating with many different people at different levels of organizational responsibility and must be sensitive to the problems as they exist, as well as be sharp enough to spot difficulties that management may not be aware of.

3. *Perception.* A consultant must be able to see beyond the considerations of others. He may run into many individuals in the organization, from management to operations, who each have his/her own conception of what problems exist and what solutions are needed. He should listen with an open mind and with the intention of gathering data, but he should look as well at what activities are actually going on and evaluate the information he obtains in light of his own training, experience, and problem solving skill. He must be able to perceive the actual situation for himself rather than to rely on the interpretations of others.

4. *Coordination.* The consultant must know as well as possible what the intention of senior management is as regards the business activity. Senior management should always have a clear goal in mind as well as a rough plan for achieving that goal. Often these goals and plans will not be stated fully in writing and the consultant will have to deal directly with persons in high management positions to determine just what direction is envisioned for the company or business even if they exist only as a vague idea in some executive's mind. He should get these goals in writing as well as how his task relates to what the company wants to achieve. In some cases, there will be so much confusion in management as to which direction the business should take, that the consultant is forced to either assist management in reaching a decision or wait until management succeeds in providing a more clear cut direction.

What to Look for in a Consultant

5. *Objectivity.* The consultant should of course not be tied to any one vendor, but also he should not be tied too closely to the business for whom he is doing the consultantcy either by financial interests or personal interests.

6. *Persistence.* The consultant should see a job through to the end without getting sidetracked by other problems or activities.

7. *Stability.* Once you begin implementing his suggestions, the consultant should be available for further consultation and troubleshooting and not be off on assignment in Hong Kong or the Bahamas.

8. *Written Contracts.* The consultant should provide and/or sign a written contract describing services to be performed. Before the consultant begins any work and before any long-range promises or major financial commitments are made, be sure to draw up a written contract describing as clearly as possible what the consultant is being hired to do. The contract should include, among other things, the time frame involved in the consulting work. Break down the overall consulting project into steps or phases and assign a completion date to each phase. Arrange consulting payments so that they occur in segments scheduled to be awarded after the completion of a particular phase of work.

   Complications may arise once the work begins and deadlines may need to be changed, but put this in writing as well. Be realistic but project yourself against paying for work that does not in fact get done.

9. *Disagreements.* Disagreements can happen. Should disagreements lead to irreconcilable differences and court proceedings seem inevitable, it would be worthwhile to have had included in any written agreement an arbitration clause. An arbitration clause should state that if any disagreements arise between the parties to the agreement, that both sides agree to submit the matter to impartial arbitration and to abide by the decision of the arbitrator. Such a clause could help avoid the time and money involved in having to bring irreconcilable disputes before the courts.

The size of the business and the amount of financial expenditure involved will of course help to determine how strictly you will want to follow each of the above points.

If you choose to employ a consultant, consideration of the key points above will help insure that your business is getting the most benefit from this type of service.

3 The Legal Environment

Word processing technology is ideally suited to the legal atmosphere. Those in the legal profession quite often have to meet high production demands within a relatively short deadline. During litigation actions, court systems usually require that the filing of documents be done within strict time limits. Failure to file proper documents within those time requirements can sometimes result in the court's refusal to accept the documents at all. In addition to having the documents filed on time, the courts require specific standards to be followed in the formatting of many documents, such as proper line spacing, correct heading information, paper size, and many other factors. It is not uncommon for a court clerk to refuse to accept for filing any document that does not meet the standards set down for his particular court district. In addition, state, federal, and municipal courts do not all have the same format requirements. To make matters worse, different courts within the same city may have completely different format requirements. This demand for strict compliance to accepted formats and adherence to set time limits makes the law profession ideally suited to the benefits of computerized word processing.

The legal profession is also one in which words wield tremendous power. The arrangement, definition, and use of words, both legalese and common English, are matters of great concern and emphasis to attorneys, legal executives and others in the legal field. The validity or not of a business contract may lie in the arrangement of a few words.

WORD PROCESSING LEGAL APPLICATIONS

The outcome of a court battle often hinges on the definition or interpretation of a few key words or terms. It is true that the pen is mightier than the sword. With the advent of the dictaphone and electronic typewriter, new weaponry was added to the legal arsenal. Today with the introduction of word processing into the legal office, space-age heavy artillery has arrived.

All the benefits of word processing in business applications apply as well to the legal environment. In the legal environment, one will find a large number of different types of documents and formats required. Some of these which could be handled on word processing equipment include:

contracts

settlements

agreements

stipulations

waivers

deeds

wills

trust documents

articles of incorporation

by-laws

affidavits

declarations

interrogatories

deposition transcripts

hearing/trial transcripts

memoranda

business letters

form letters

resumes

pleadings

case summaries

exhibits

graphs/charts

billing forms

case file indexes

client lists

mailing lists

case summaries

special briefings

patent/trademark/copyright applications

Some of the advantages of word processing to the legal office environment include:

Advantages of Word Processing

1. *Less time spent typing by the legal secretary.* The secretary will be involved usually in typing the *first* draft of pleadings only as the revision work will be done in word processing. This leaves more time for the secretaries to devote to other matters.

2. *Faster turnaround time for revisions.* With word processing equipment one can make revisions and reprint entire pages in a matter of minutes.

3. *Less proofreading time by attorneys.* Since revisions can be made to portions of a document without having to retype the whole document, proofreading can be limited on the second draft to checking those new revisions only. The word processing department can also take on a great deal of the proofreading duties either through individual operators or by having a specially assigned proofreader who performs this function full time.

4. *Higher quality work product at less cost.* Many of the professional, letter quality printers available with word processing systems are capable of producing greater resolution of characters and better uniformity of text than electric typewriters and output at far greater speed. Printers can also be shared by several WP terminals run full time, thus producing more printed text per hour than even two or more electric typewriters.

5. *Creation of standard document library.* Word processing storage can be utilized to store many different standard formats for letters, agreements, and pleadings which can be modified and reprinted very easily.

6. *Use of boilerplate clauses.* The term boilerplate refers to a clause or phrase or a series of paragraphs which are relatively standard in construction and are used over and over again in various types of documents, often with only minor variations. Boilerplate text can be stored in a WP system and simply retrieved and input into the text of any contract or agreement where appropriate. This is not only faster than retyping the text each time, but allows for greater accuracy since the wording of the text can be drafted and approved and used as a standard format time and again. Use of

boilerplate clauses thus helps prevent errors or omissions that might enter in if the material had to be re-input each time it was needed.

Legal Fees/ Billings to Clients

Most law firms operate on a financial system revolving around the amount of time an attorney or assistant spends on a particular client's legal problem. This time is referred to as *billable hours*. A large part of the accounting work in a law firm involves the recording, verifying, and calculating of billings to clients for work done by the firm.

The client's bill is determined by multiplying the billable hours times the hourly rate which the firm charges for that particular attorney or assistant's time. For example, an attorney's time may be charged at an hourly rate of $140 per hour. If he spends six hours working on a legal matter for client X, the bill would be calculated as follows:

Billable Hours	Times	Hourly Rate	Total
6	×	$140.00	= $840.00

For the client's information, the bills are often itemized, for example:

CLIENT: Mr. J. Jones   FILE NO.: 01001

DATE	ACTIVITY	HOURS
7/2/84	Law research	1.5
7/3/84	Phone conference with Mr. Jones	.5
7/6/84	Preparation of defense papers and reply memorandum	3.0
7/7/84	Attendance at preliminary hearing	1.0
	Total Billable Hours =	6.00

At first glance this may look simple but things get more involved. Not all time spent by an attorney is billable time. Careful records must be kept as to how much time is actually spent on a client's legal matter. Also, an attorney will probably have more than one client's work in progress at the same time. More importantly, the hourly rate which a law firm charges for its attorneys differs among the various attorneys, based on their experience, seniority, and expertise in a given field of law. There are different types of legal support staff too, and these may be billed out at different hourly rates. Some of these include:

law clerks

paralegals

word processors

legal messengers

In addition, a law firm may utilize outside attorneys, accounting firms, or investigative agencies during the course of its work on a particular client's project. The expenses for all of these have to be carefully monitored and taken into consideration when computing the client's monthly bill. Therefore, for law firms larger than eight or ten attorneys the process of compiling the client billings can become a massive data collection and tabulation task. The storing of data concerning billable hours on a computer/word processing system can help alleviate this problem especially in firms where there is a local area network with a central data storage facility. Some firms produce all their client billings internally while others utilize outside professional billing services. Whichever method is used, there is still a certain amount of individual record keeping by each attorney and legal support staff as regards billable hours. Before the final bill is sent to the client, it is usually reviewed by the attorney for correctness and completeness and may be subject to last minute revisions. There should exist some internal facilities for the last minute correction of client billings so time is not wasted in having to send them out of the office for small changes.

With billing information stored on internal word/information processing equipment it becomes possible to generate specialized reports such as breakdown reports of all billable hours listed by attorney, financial status reports, year-end gross profit and loss statements, summaries of predicted income and expenses, and many other reports that may be helpful in the overall management of the law firm or legal office.

LEGAL DOCUMENT PROCESSING

Many legal documents go through a large number of revisions before being finalized. Word processing technology allows for numerous revisions with much greater speed and accuracy than previously available using only electric/electronic typewriters.

Court Requirements

An invaluable item which the legal word processor should have as part of his/her administrative tools is a listing of the special formats required by the various courts he/she will be dealing with. Some courts require single spacing on footnotes, for example, where others require double spacing. Some require that all documents submitted be typed on ruled and numbered paper, while others require plain white paper. These and many other requirements are also subject to change by the court so the legal word processor will need to keep up in communication with the attorneys/legal secretaries/paralegals working on the various cases to ensure that products are produced in a format acceptable to the court.

Standard Intraoffice Formats

Another challenge facing the legal word processor is the myriad of document variations sometimes requested by in-house users. In some legal environments, each attorney/legal executive has his/her own preference for formatting legal text, headings, pagination, footnotes, etc. Some wise legal executives have conquered this time consuming problem by having an internal "standard formats manual" to which all documents produced by that firm/office must conform. Such a manual is not only a time and aggravation saver, but allows the office and the word processing department to produce a uniform high quality product according to agreed upon standards and enables the word processing personnel to spot and correct variations from the agreed upon standard. This is not to say, of course, that all documents must look alike, but is to say that arbitrary formats should be standardized within any legal environment to avoid confusion and wasted production time.

Telecommunications

Some of the legal documents that may go through many drafts include "articles of incorporation" and "by-laws" being formulated for new or established corporations. Whole paragraphs can be added, deleted or moved about within the documents with a minimum amount of effort and time involved. With the added speed of a telecommunications modem, documents can be drafted by a law firm in New York, for example, and relayed from a WP terminal over the phone lines to the data processing department of a major corporation in Dallas for review by its corporate officers. Any required changes can then be communicated back to the attorneys at the firm and the document redrafted accordingly. With such a setup, the documents can go through a large number of drafts until a finalized form is agreed upon. All this can take place without the document ever hitting the printer. Once the revisions are completed, the document can then be printed in final form, one time. This can be a great savings in terms of corporate executive time, attorney time and legal expenses, and of course paper.

Litigation, the process of bringing an action or dispute before the courts for judicial determination, is an area of law that provides a great opportunity for the full use of word processing technology.

Litigation can be likened to a fencing contest between two or more masters where each thrust is designed to strike deeper into the opposition's position and each parry is designed to be more effective than the last. Ideally, one would wish to dispatch an opponent with as few strokes as possible and come out completely unscathed. In practice, this is usually easier said than done. Where the pen takes the place of the sword, the thrusts and parries take the form of legal pleadings—complaints, replies, cross-complaints, legal arguments, supporting memoranda, etc.

Effective legal pleadings require a high degree of expertise not only in drafting the arguments themselves, but in assembling the finished product. Correct grammar and spelling are vital. There are also various technical standards which must be met for each level of court or district to which the pleading is being submitted for review. For example, references to prior court decisions must follow a format which has become more or less standard throughout the legal profession. The "bible" for such standard representation of citations is a handbook called *A Uniform System of Citation* published and distributed by the Harvard Law Review Association. This 240 (or so) page handbook usually has a blue cover and has become known in the legal field as the *Harvard Blue Book*. An example of a correct citation would look something like this:

Jefferson v. Maddison, 341 F. Supp. 333 (N.D. Cal. 1974).

Roughly translated, the above citation tells you that

Jefferson brought suit against Maddison

the results of the case were reported in the Federal Supplement (F. Supp.) (a multi-volume record of decisions reached in federal court cases.)

it is in volume *341* of the Federal Supplement at page *333*

the case was heard in the United States District Court for the Northern District of California

the case was decided in 1974

There are *many* different forms that citations can take. Failing to abide by certain standards, such as those set forth in the *Harvard Blue Book,* can cause a great deal of confusion and lack of communication. Some law firms have their own internal standards for citations but the Blue Book is the most widely recognized. The Blue Book, therefore, is one of the vital tools of a word processor in the legal environment.

WORD PROCESSING BACKUP FOR THE LITIGATOR

Although the legal word processor is not responsible for citing the correct supporting cases for the arguments being presented, he must have a working knowledge of the correct format for citations so as to spot and correct errors in usage as well as typographical errors.

CALENDARING OF IMPORTANT DATES

Word processing equipment can be utilized to keep a list of all key dates such as court hearings, trials, meetings, filing dates, deposition schedules, etc. If attorneys or secretaries have terminals at their disposal which have access to a common storage facility, they can update the calendar file immediately whenever situations change. In this way, any attorney or support staff in the office can access a full listing of all the important court and meeting dates and determine where conflicts may arise or establish when certain personnel will be out of the office on what days and where they can be found. It may also be useful in locating times when attorneys will be available for scheduling future meetings.

A sample page of a typical in-house calendar is seen in the following section (Figure 3-8).

SAMPLE LEGAL FORMATS

Figures 3-1 through 3-11 show sample formats for various types of legal documents. Some documents, such as pleadings, are filed with a court or judicial body. Others, such as memoranda, agenda and board minutes are often used in-house by the attorneys or office staff themselves.

The documents shown are typical examples of legal formats. Variations of the formats shown are possible within the guidelines of the respective courts, or in the case of in-house documents, according to the accepted office standards.

Some legal offices may store certain formats such as caption pages, board minutes and proof of service on a word processing storage medium (such as diskette or hard disk) and use these as *masters* or *boilerplate* documents. These boilerplate documents can then be copied and conformed to a specific legal case or matter at hand. This saves a great deal of time and helps to provide uniformity and correctness of style.

LEGAL RESEARCH

Attorneys and paralegals may want to use word processing equipment as an aid to storing legal research memoranda, case law, and indexes of relevant cases. This data can then be searched at a later time to determine if a particular point of law is covered. Such a system could possibly be used in connection with LEXIS®, a computerized legal re-

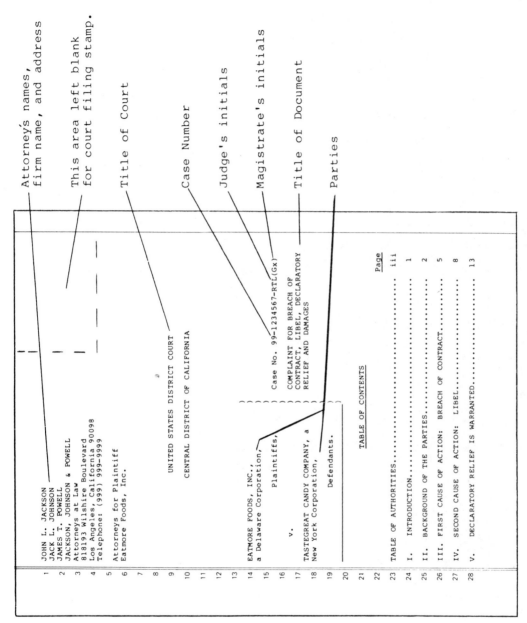

Figure 3-1. Sample caption page for legal pleading United States District Court.

TABLE OF CONTENTS

Figure 3-2. Table of Contents

TABLE OF AUTHORITIES

Page

Cases:

Federal Statutes:

State Statutes:

Other Authorities:

- iii -

Figure 3-3. Table of Authorities

1	<u>MEMORANDUM OF POINTS AND AUTHORITIES</u>
2	I
3	<u>INTRODUCTION</u>
4	Court requirements for legal documents may vary in
5	several respects. Most courts will require double spacing
6	of all typed text, while others require single spacing of
7	footnotes<u>1/</u> and lengthy quotes.
8	"This is a sample of a single-spaced, blocked
	and indented quote. Such quotes are blocked
9	and indented to set them off from the rest of
	the text and single spaced to take up less
10	space on the page."
11	This sample page is typed on 8-1/2 x 11 inch legal-lined
12	or "ruled and numbered" paper consisting of 28 numbered lines.
13	Some courts require that all pleadings be submitted on ruled and
14	numbered paper, others prefer plain white paper. The numbers
15	on the left margin provide quick reference pointers to a
16	specific line or lines of text within a document and also make
17	it more difficult to make unauthorized changes to a legal
18	document once it has been printed in final form.
19	* * * *
20	* * * *
21	* * * *
22	* * * *
23	* * * *
24	_____
25	<u>1/</u> Legal documents may contain numerous footnotes
	requiring proper formatting, numbering and placement
26	in alignment with the text. In the legal environment,
	word processing equipment with the capability to handle
27	footnotes becomes very important. Automatic footnote
	handling is a feature that will save legal word processors
28	much time in having to reformat footnotes manually when
	text is added or deleted.

Figure 3-4. Sample page of a legal document
showing several of the common formats used.

```
 1  JOHN P. LYONS
    WILLIAM A. DUVAL
 2  ATTORNEYS AT LAW
    81924 W. 37th Street
 3  Los Angeles, California  90019

 4  Attorneys for Plaintiff
    Polychemical Sales, Inc.

 5

 6

 7

 8               UNITED STATES DISTRICT COURT

 9               CENTRAL DISTRICT OF CALIFORNIA

10

11  Polychemical Sales, Inc.     )
    a California corporation,     )
12                               )
              Plaintiffs,         )
13                               )  No. 84-345211-RMG(Kd)
          v.                      )
14                               )  [PROPOSED]
    Universal Electroplating      )  ORDER GRANTING PLAINTIFF'S
15  Industries, a New Jersey      )  MOTION FOR PRELIMINARY
    Corporation,                  )  INJUNCTION
16                               )
              Defendants.         )
17  _____)

18        Plaintiff's Motion for Preliminary Injunction came

19  on for hearing by the court on this date.  Having read the facts

20  before it and having heard the arguments of counsel both for and

21  against--

22  IT IS HEREBY ORDERED that plaintiff's Motion for Preliminary

23  Injunction, dated June 23, 1986, be and hereby is granted; and

24  IT IS FURTHER ORDERED that defendants are to pay the costs of

25  this motion and hearing.

26

27  DATED:  _____        _____
                                    District Court Judge
28
```

Figure 3-5. Proposed Order

PROOF OF SERVICE BY MAIL

(Federal Court)

STATE OF CALIFORNIA, COUNTY OF LOS ANGELES:

I am employed in the County of Los Angeles, State of California; I am over the age of 18 and not a party to the within action; my business address is _____, Los Angeles, California _____.

On _____ , 1986, I served the parties in this action by placing a true copy of "[EXACT TITLE OF DOCUMENT BEING FILED]" enclosed in a sealed envelope, with postage thereon fully prepaid, in the United States mail at Los Angeles, California, addressed as follows:

> John P. Lyons, Esq.
> William A. Duval, Esq.
> ATTORNEYS AT LAW
> 81924 W. 37th Street
> Los Angeles, California 90015

I declare that I am employed in the office of a member of the bar of this Court at whose direction the service was made.

Executed on _____ , 1986, at Los Angeles, California.

_____
(signature)

Figure 3-6. Proof of Service

78

SETTLEMENT AGREEMENT AND MUTUAL RELEASE

This Settlement Agreement and Mutual Release (hereinafter "Agreement") is entered into as follows:

A. PARTIES.

The parties to this agreement are:

1. TASTEGREAT CANDY COMPANY, a Delaware Corporation; and

2. EATMORE FOODS, INC., a New Jersey Corporation.

B. SUBJECT MATTER OF THE AGREEMENT.

1. This agreement arises from the claims asserted in the lawsuit entitled Tastegreat Candy Co. vs. Eatmore Foods, Inc., Case No. 98743981, filed in the New Jersey Superior Court on January 5, 1985 (hereinafter "Litigation").

2. This Agreement concerns the release of any and all causes of action, claims, demands, rights and damages of whatever kind which exist or may arise against EATMORE FOODS, INC.

C. CONSIDERATION.

1. In consideration for dismissal of the Litigation with prejudice and the relinquishment of all claims against EATMORE FOODS, INC., EATMORE FOODS, INC. agrees to pay TASTEGREAT CANDY COMPANY the amount of $5,000.00 on or before February 25, 1987.

Figure 3-7(a). Settlement Agreement

D.   RELEASES.

       1.   The TASTEGREAT CANDY COMPANY hereby releases and
discharges EATMORE FOODS, INC. and its agents and employees from
any and all claims, causes of action, demands, rights and
damages which they had or which they may have developed or
alleged in the Litigation.

E.   APPLICABLE LAW.

       This Agreement shall be governed by and interpreted
according to the laws of the State of New Jersey.

F.   EFFECTIVE DATE.

       This Effective Date of this Agreement is February
25, 1987.

DATED: February ___, 1987.   TASTEGREAT CANDY CO.

                                     By _____
                                        President
                                        Tastegreat Candy Co.

DATED: February ___, 1987.   EATMORE FOODS, INC.

                                     By _____
                                        President
                                        Eatmore Foods, Inc.

[Word processing diskette reference,
      if applicable]   [Date of printing
                                          this draft]

[TKL23]   1/12/87
                        - 2 -

Figure 3-7(b). Settlement Agreement

80

LICHTER, ZIMMERMAN & McKENNA

ATTORNEYS AT LAW

Intra-Office

C A L E N D A R

January 3, 1987 -- January 31, 1987

DATE	ATTORNEYS	CASE/SUBJECT MATTER
January 3, 1987 -- THURSDAY --	HJK/RKZ	SAMPSON v. HARRISON - Last day to file reply to Harrison's counterclaim of 11/25/86
	RKZ	RASKIN v. THOMPSON - Meeting with R. Jackson, 9:30 a.m., at offices of Jackson, Jackson & Levy, 93491 Wilshire Boulevard, Suite 3009, to discuss RASKIN settlement offer
January 4, 1987 -- FRIDAY --	RKZ/TLB	PERKINS ESTATE - Last day for Mrs. Perkins to object to executor's decision
	HJK/RKZ	PETERS v. LANGHAM - Hearing on Peters' motion for summary judgment, U.S. District Court, courtroom 12, 10:00 a.m.
	HJK	SAMUELS (Property Claims) - Meeting with M. Samuels, here, 9:30 a.m.
January 7, 1987 -- MONDAY --	HKJ/RKZ/ TLB/RTC/ RLT/CBD	Firm Meeting, 12:00 Noon, Vanderbilt Ballroom, Westin-Regency Hotel, 112 W. Ninth St.; lunch at 12:45
	RLT/CBD	A.E.G.I.S. v. R.T.C., Inc. - Last day to file motion charging defendants with violation of court orders and application for sanctions

- page one -

Figure 3-8. Intra-Office Calendar

```
 1 |                        VERIFICATION
   |
 2 | STATE OF CALIFORNIA, COUNTY OF _____
   |
 3 |          I, the undersigned, say:
   |
 4 |          I am a party to this action.  I have read the
   |
 5 | foregoing _____
   |
 6 | _____
   |
 7 | _____ and know its contents.  The matters in it are
   |
 8 | true of my own knowledge, except as to those matters which are
   |
 9 | stated upon information and belief, and as to those matters I
   |
10 | believe them to be true.
   |
11 |          I declare under penalty of perjury that the above is
   |
12 | true and correct.
   |
13 |          Executed on _____, 1984, at _____,
   |
14 | California.
   |
15 |
   |
16 |                            _____
   |
17 |
18 |
19 |
20 |
21 |
22 |
23 |
24 |
25 |
26 |
27 |
28 |
```

Figure 3-9. Verification Form

MINUTES OF MEETING OF THE BOARD OF DIRECTORS OF

TECHNO-CHEMICAL PRODUCTS CORPORATION

WE, THE UNDERSIGNED, being all the members of the board of Techno-Chemical Products Corporation as presently constituted, having met and reviewed all matters pending, hereby find and resolve as follows:

WHEREAS: Sales in the San Francisco Office have dropped considerably and consistently over the past two years; and

WHEREAS: The lease for the San Francisco Office has expired and there are no options for lease renewal; and

WHEREAS: There has been an increasing demand for raw chemicals in the San Diego area;

IT IS HEREBY RESOLVED: That effective October 25, 1986, the San Francisco Office will be closed and all personnel, material, and related supplies will be moved to San Diego for establishment of an office in that city.

IT IS FURTHER RESOLVED: That the Vice President of Operations is hereby given full authority for the relocation operations and is hereby required to report to this Board concerning the progress of the relocation operations on a weekly basis until completed.

There being no further business to be discussed, the meeting was adjourned.   DATED: _____

_____   _____

_____   _____

_____   _____

(signatures)   (signatures)

Figure 3-10.   Corporate Board Minutes

JACOBS, GRAYSON & FREDERICKS

ATTORNEYS AT LAW

_____

M E M O R A N D U M

TO: Ted Grayson

FROM: K. Dorian   DATE: 9/24/86

CC: Files   FILE NO.:   94587AA

Re: ANALYSIS OF BAKER V. SAMUELS CASE

PARTIES: [--------------------------]

SUMMARY OF CASE: [--]
[---]
[---]

ISSUES INVOLVED: [--]
[---]
[---]

QUESTIONS OF LAW: [---]
[---]
[---]

QUESTIONS OF FACT: [--]
[---]
[---]

ARGUMENTS: [--]
[---]
[---]

DOCUMENTARY EVIDENCE NEEDED: [--------------------------------]
[---]
[---]
[---]
[---]

KLD:jb
[JH5]

Figure 3-11. Legal Menu

search service developed by Mead Data Central. LEXIS is a service that one is billed for. When doing research on LEXIS for a particular client, the cost of the research time is quite often passed on directly to the client. LEXIS would become an expense to the law firm itself if the research being done is not for any particular client, but for some other purpose. In-house files of legal research done could be stored on word processing equipment and retrieved for further use at a later time at no additional cost to the firm.

There are various options available in word processing systems but not all systems will have equal capabilities in all areas. Figure 3-12 is an example of one word processing system designed for legal word processing capabilities. One of the options to look for in a word processor for legal documents is the capability to automatically handle footnotes. Many legal documents will have to include numerous footnotes and the ability of the equipment to automatically handle these is very important. In automatic footnote handling the footnotes would be inserted into the text at the proper location, i.e., on the same page as the footnote reference. When the document is revised, the footnote should automatically be positioned to "track" with the appropriate footnote reference. This is often referred to as footnote tracking. If a footnote is added or deleted, the footnote numbers are automatically adjusted up or down accordingly.

WORD PROCESSING EQUIPMENT FOR LEGAL WORK

Some other important word processing options to look for in equipment that will be used for legal document work are:

Automatic page numbering. Since legal documents will often go through a large number of revisions, you will want a word processor with the ability to automatically renumber all the pages of a document after changes have been made.

Global Search and Search & Replace. This function will allow an entire document to be searched for a particular word, phrase or symbol in a matter of minutes and if needed, replace that word, phrase or symbol with other data.

Automatic Table of Contents generation/Automatic Table of Authorities generation. Legal pleadings will often have both a Table of Contents and a Table of Authorities (see Appendix D, LEGAL GLOSSARY). The ability to "generate" or pull out the needed information from the text of a document automatically will save a great deal of time in preparing such tables.

Document Assembly. This function allows you to integrate portions of two or more different documents into a single document. This is useful in combining a lengthy series of questions filed by one party with the responses being submitted by the other party, and results in a single document with both questions and responses.

Figure 3-12. The Barrister Word Processing
System is designed for legal word processing
applications. A range of system configurations are
available for law firms of all sizes. Shown here is the
Barrister System 150, a compact and
environmentally advanced CPU which can easily fit
into the office setting. The 150 supports Barrister's
word processing software as well as other
specialized law office applications, including:
financial management, litigation support, spread
sheet applications, and information management.
*(Photo courtesy of Barrister Information Systems
Corporation.)*

Split Screen/Windowing. Some advanced systems have the capability to split the viewing screen into two or more segments or
"windows" allowing the operator to view portions of two or more documents simultaneously which aids greatly in document assembly.

Automatic Document Reformatting. If you delete a page or
series of paragraphs, you may want the system to automatically
reformat the entire document to absorb the blank spaces and merge
paragraphs appropriately.

Dictionary/Spelling Option. Some systems have the ability to
search a document for misspelled words, whether English or specialized terminology. The system flags these for your correction. This
may be a helpful aid in some working environments, but should not
be used as a substitute for careful proofing of finalized documents.

The legal environment puts perhaps the greatest demand on a WP operator's technical and administrative skills. One will usually find the highest demand for proficient operators in this area. Consequently, the salaries and benefits for WP operators usually are higher on the average in law related applications. Having some legal training, such as legal secretarial or paralegal, in addition to word processing skills is an added bonus, but it is usually not mandatory.

OPERATOR SKILL

The product produced by a legal word processor can be briefly stated as: High quality, professional looking legal documents correctly typed, formatted, and assembled with both speed and accuracy.

PRODUCT OF A LEGAL WORD PROCESSOR

A typical listing of materials the legal word processor operator might find of great assistance include:

ADMINISTRATIVE SUPPLIES FOR WORD PROCESSORS IN LEGAL OFFICE WORK

Black's Law Dictionary West Publishing Co.	For correct spelling and definitions of legal terms (This is the most authoritative and complete legal dictionary.)
The Legal Secretary's Encyclopedic Dictionary 3rd Edition Prentice-Hall Editorial Staff rev. Mary A. Devries	For easy to understand explanations of key terms and their usage (with illustrations)
Directories of Attorneys/Law Firms	To check for correct spelling of names and addresses of other attorneys/firms [these are usually published by area]
A Uniform System of Citation (*Harvard Blue Book*)	For correct usage of citations
A standard formats manual	For internal office format standards [where available]
A listing of phone numbers for telecommunications equipment of clients and sister offices	Specialized for each firm/office and includes any needed equipment specifications for proper two-way communication

Martindale-Hubbell Directory	A multi-volume directory listing all the attorneys admitted to state bars in the U.S. and includes some foreign attorneys (Usually available in law libraries or large law firms)
Master library of various forms	Such as: proof of service forms verifications settlement agreements waivers contracts etc.
List of active cases or current clients by file number.	For cross-checking for correct spelling of client names, correct file numbers, etc.
(and last, but not least) Professional Word Processing in Business and Legal Environments Reston Publishing Company	As a guide to legal word processing skills, specialized formats, WP and legal terminology, reference sources, etc.

SAMPLE JOB DESCRIPTION

TITLE: WORD PROCESSING SPECIALIST—LEGAL:

PURPOSE:

To support the legal services delivered by the firm/corporation by producing high quality, professional looking legal documents which are technically correct as to format, grammar, punctuation, spelling, citations, and other standards through the use of electronic text editing equipment and related technical and reference manuals.

DUTIES:

1. Completes text revision of complex legal documents.

2. Correctly formats.

3. Proofreads carefully.

4. Checks correctness of legal citations and other legal formats in accordance with accepted legal standards by various court districts.

5. Assumes full responsibility for accuracy and completeness of own work.

6. Performs proper information storage and retrieval functions.

7. Correctly operates telecommunications modems.

8. Correctly uses OCR (optical character reader) equipment.

9. Fills in as overflow typist when needed.

10. Maintains and improves knowledge of advances within the word processing field, including state-of-the-art equipment, high speed printers, improvements in editing features, magnetic storage and related word processing support equipment.

11. Applies proper diskette care and storage.

12. Maintains adequate security regarding confidential documents or projects.

13. Organizes work flows to allow for priorities and heavy work loads.

14. Maintains and improves transcription skills.

15. Maintains log of work completed.

16. Keeps in communication with current vendor in regard to word processing supplies and new developments.

17. Sees that any equipment breakdowns are rapidly reported to service personnel and handled.

18. Sees that in-house equipment maintenance and cleaning is kept up adequately.

19. Correctly routes or has routed the finished products so that they arrive in the hands of the user.

MINIMUM QUALIFICATIONS REQUIRED:

1. Two years of word processing experience.

2. One year of legal office experience.

3. Excellent grammar, spelling, punctuation, and word usage skills.

4. Minimum typing speed of 65 w.p.m.

5. Accurate transcription skills.

6. Familiarity with OCR and telecommunications equipment.

7. Familiarity with legal and secretarial reference materials.

8. Ability to produce high quality products consistently.

9. Ability to work with others effectively.

10. Ability to work under pressure and meet necessary production demands.

EXAMPLE OF FLOW LINES TO AND FROM WP DEPART-MENT

Figure 3-13 is a block diagram showing the course a typical legal document might follow from start to finish.

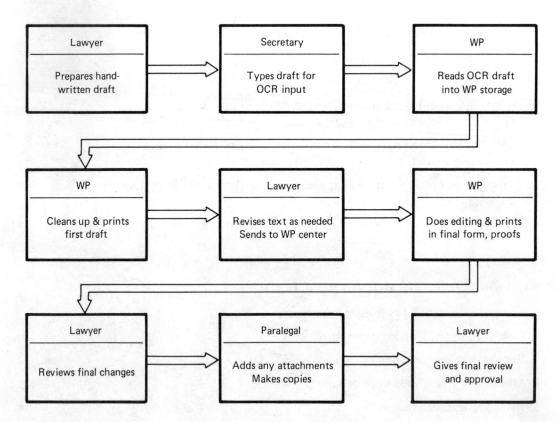

Figure 3-13.   Course of a Typical Legal Document

4

Choosing and Setting Up a Word Processing System

To get the most for your money, a thorough review of your information processing needs should be done prior to purchasing or leasing or even examining any word processing equipment. To accomplish such a review does not necessarily require teams of outside consultants and pages and pages of cost analysis, etc. If your demand for information processing is very large, such as in a bank or large corporation or legal office, then outside professional consultants may be able to do a better and faster job of determining what type of system you will best profit by. Where the information processing demands are not as great, but are still significant, in-house managerial and administrative personnel should be able to determine at least how much work a word processing system will have to process internally to fill the needs of the office. Consultants may be of assistance here, too, but your own internal management should be very much aware of the present and future needs of the office in terms of document processing and overall office automation. Otherwise, consultancy time is partially consumed in determining what problems exist rather than in assisting in best solving those problems. If a word processing/data processing department already exists in your business, the supervisory personnel and terminal operators are the best source of information regarding current work loads, adequacy or inadequacy of the equipment in use, needed improvements, ergonomic problems, production backlogs, space and equipment utilization and many other relevant factors based on their firsthand, day-to-day experience.

CENTRALIZATION vs. DECENTRALIZATION

Centralization

CENTRALIZATION is the term used to describe a system configuration where all the electronic equipment and support personnel for a particular activity, such as word processing, are located in a central location. In a centralized service environment, support personnel have their own supervisors and are not directly under the authority of any one user. Many different users could have access to a centralized word/data processing service.

Some of the advantages of centralization are:

1. *Cost reduction.* In a centralized environment, the word processing systems can be set up to share various peripheral devices such as printers, OCR readers, storage devices and even CPU's.

2. *Environment control.* In very large installations, room temperature and air quality are important to the optimum performance of the more delicate electronic equipment. In a centralized environment, this is much easier to achieve. Security over files and storage media is also easier to maintain with all this information centrally located.

3. *Noise reduction.* Where printers are involved, it is possible to have special soundproofing arrangements set up to control noise levels in a particular location. In a decentralized environment, however, printers are often distributed throughout an office and noise reduction methods have to be employed on an individual basis. These can be more costly and less effective in keeping overall noise levels of the office down to comfortable levels.

4. *Personnel utilization.* With all the word processing personnel located in a central location, work loads can be more easily handled for optimum utilization of personnel.

5. *Quality control.* Supervisory personnel will be better able to maintain overall quality control over the products being produced by direct inspection.

6. *Training.* Training of new word processing operators and enhancement of current personnel can be accomplished during normal working hours and under direct supervision without a loss of production or distraction to other personnel. The centralized environment also fosters an atmosphere of professionalism which leads also to greater pride in one's work and better products.

The Case for Decentralization

Despite all the seeming advantages of centralization, there may exist certain working conditions that are best suited to decentralized word processing. An example of this situation is in an office where each user requires full-time use of a particular word processing secretary involving specialized skills or aspects of work that do not directly involve other employees in the same office. In such a situation, it may be more cost effective to have several independently stationed word processing secretaries, each with specialized skills for a particular area, set up in their own work stations and under the direct supervision of the executive for whom the work is being done. This saves the time and expense of having to train numerous operators on various skills to accommodate many different users. Also, the turnaround time in some office situations may be so crucial that users cannot afford the few extra minutes it may take to get a delivery from a word processing center down the hall, or across the street or wherever it may be. In addition to the above, in some cases the executive may wish to have word processing or personal computing equipment in his/her own office for personal day-to-day handling of business matters. Getting one to give up this luxury may not prove so easy.

UTILIZATION SURVEY

Some factors to consider in establishing a word processing system or expanding a current system include:

1. Is your office/business expanding, contracting or stable?
2. What equipment exists now (including typewriters, dictaphones, word processors, etc.) and how well is it utilized?
3. What effect does an unexpected increase in production demand have upon the staff?
4. Are current staff adequately trained on the equipment presently in use?
5. Where do the lines of production snarl up?
6. What production backlogs occur and where?

7. Does any of the equipment fail to operate correctly under increased demand?

8. Are any staff under utilized?

9. Do personnel problems exist?

10. Is there equipment standing idle?

    If so, is it because:

    a. it's outdated?

    b. it's broken?

    c. it's simply not required, or

    d. no one knows how to use it?

11. Is there a high percentage of downtime with your current system?

12. How does your equipment vendor respond to emergency service calls?

13. Is your office equipped with a large number of different types of word processing equipment, each with its own capabilities, shortfalls, and vendors?

14. Does your accounting department adequately interface with other information processing units within your business?

    If not,

    a. should it have to?

    b. is it already successfully operating as it stands?

15. Are there no major problems or barriers to current production, but only a desire to increase future productivity?

If the above items are examined honestly one by one, by the time you reach number 15 it should be very easy to spot where the major production difficulties lie and what areas need further attention and improvement. Be sure to distinguish between a **minor problem** and a **major problem.** An insufficient number of dictating machines is a minor problem and is easily corrected. A whole batch of electronic typewriters that consistently break down, combined with slow service response is a major problem that is costing you money. One staff member who refuses to read and follow standard office policy on correct memo format and internal routings is a minor problem. A complete lack of any such policy is a major omission and could be the cause of other problems. Disrupting an activity or department that is already functioning correctly and adequately to institute "improvements" may be an error and could cause a temporary decrease in production, and upset personnel who felt that they were doing their job correctly.

Different types of word processing systems vary as to their capabilities, speed, reliability, cost, and size. In choosing a word processing system or a single unit there are a number of things to consider. These include:

1. *Cost.* How much do you want to spend? Determining this first will help narrow the field considerably. If, for example, you are limited to $6,000 for a standalone word processor and a printer, don't expect to find all the fancy options that will be available on the $12,000 and $20,000 systems.

2. *Dedicated System or PC/Microcomputer.* There are major differences between them. See Chapter 1 again for a discussion of these two types.

3. *Available Options.* Just what can the machine do for you? There are many basic options and many advanced options. Study the features available and determine if the machine has the options that you will need. Here are a few of the features you may find, but there are *many* others including math packages and data base capabilities. Consult one of the many buyer's guides available before you go shopping for a word processor, especially if you are not familiar with all the terminology.

automatic footnote tracking	puts footnotes in their proper places
automatic hyphenation	hyphenates word at the end of a line automatically
automatic page numbering	numbers and renumbers pages automatically
automatic sorting	can arrange files or other data in alphabetical or numerical order, or according to a specified code such as a zip code
block & line move	moves a block or a line of text from one point in the text to another point
justification	automatically adjusts inter-word spacing on each line to even out the right margin of text
spelling/dictionary	a WP option consisting of an internal dictionary and the capability to search text for mispelled words and flag them for correction

word wraparound   functions like an automatic carriage return
                       when you reach the end of a line and al-
                       lows you to continue typing on the line
                       immediately following

4. *Vendor Service & Assistance.* How good is the service contract? How
    reliable is the vendor? If possible, ask someone who has pur-
    chased equipment from that vendor.

5. *Compatibility & Upgrade Potential.* What other systems, software, or
    equipment is the machine compatible with? Can it be upgraded
    and how—and for how much?

There will almost certainly be other considerations that will be involved depending on your exact word processing requirements.
Choose carefully, as it will be a big investment.

EXAMPLES OF POSSIBLE SYSTEM CONFIGURA-TIONS

Figures 4-1 through 4-7 show possible system configurations.

Figure 4-1. Single Standalone Station with Printer

Figure 4-2.   Single Standalone Station with
Printer and OCR Scanner

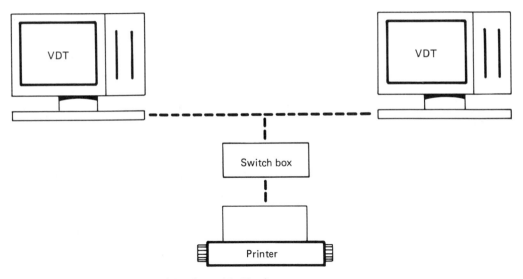

Figure 4-3. Dual Terminal Station with Single Printer

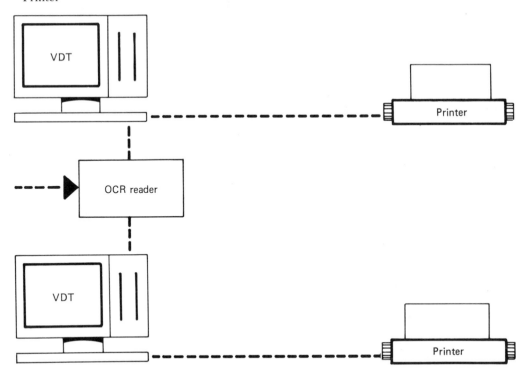

Figure 4-4. Dual Terminal Station with Two Printers and OCR Capability

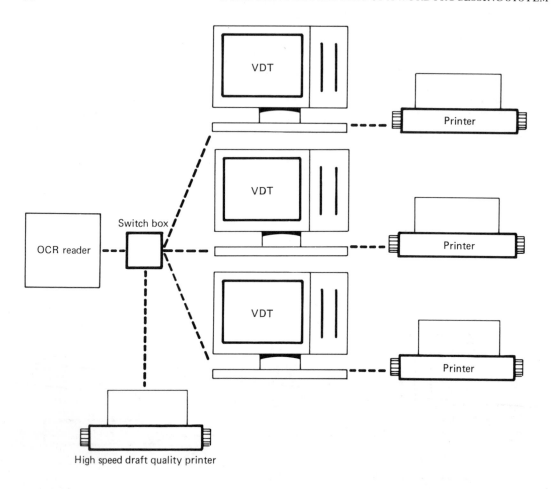

Figure 4-5.   Three Terminal System with OCR
and High Speed Output Capability

ERGONOMICS: THE "HUMAN FACTOR" IN OFFICE AUTOMATION

With more and more people spending greater amounts of time in front of word processing and/or computer terminals, the need for greater emphasis on "interfacing" various types of electronic equipment with human operators has become a recognizable factor in the design and manufacture of office equipment and in the construction and layout of today's automated office setting.

Ergonomics is the study of the relationship between human comfort, efficiency, and performance in interaction with electronic equipment. Ergonomics encompasses a great deal more than just concern over VDT glare or having the proper chair height. Perhaps the two

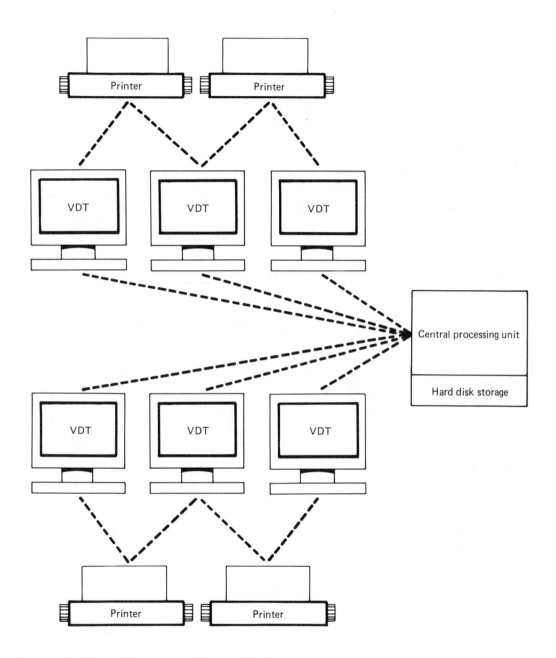

Figure 4-6. Central Processing Unit with Hard
Disk Storage and Six (Dumb) Terminals and
Shared Printers

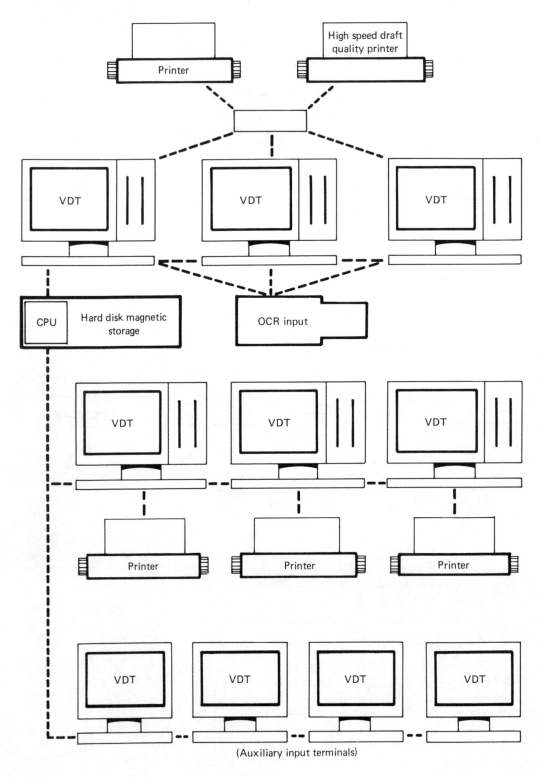

Figure 4-7. Large Scale System with Central Processing Unit and Hard Disk Storage

key factors which make ergonomics a valid concern to management and operations staff are *safety* and *production*. Under the safety category we find the need for concern that the office environment does not contain factors which would cause or contribute to health problems or excessive weariness. Electrical power cords and interfacing cables running this way and that all over the floor is an obvious safety hazard. Schedules for VDT operators that call for long hours of continuous operation with infrequent work breaks could be a factor that might contribute to eye strain and other physical complaints. Other detrimental factors include excessive office noise, poor air quality, excessive heat or cold, overcrowding, broken or ill-fitting office furniture, and even excess clutter or waste.

One example of a factor that can cause excessive weariness is incorrect lighting. Lighting can obviously be too bright or too dim. However, lighting can also be incorrectly positioned so as to cause eye strain or it can be too harsh for the office setting. At first glance many office settings may look clean and acceptable, but it should be noted that those who work in that setting are exposed to those same surroundings for 8 hours a day or more, day after day. The end-of-the-day weariness familiar to many may be due in no small part to long term exposure to a working environment containing numerous factors contributing to physical and mental tiredness. Such factors can be handled for the most part with proper equipment design and office layout. (See Figures 4-8 and 4-9.)

The importance of the second key factor, production, follows logically from the discussion above. If the work environment is comfortable rather than tiresome, aesthetic rather than sterile, and pleasant rather than harsh, then it is likely to be more conducive to production. The energy of the staff is not drained by the surroundings but can be focussed more easily towards accomplishment of the tasks at hand.

Manufacturers have recently been designing office equipment with the "human factor" in mind. Non-glare, swivel screens are available on some models of word processing equipment as well as detached keyboards for more comfortable positioning. The design and manufacture of ergonomic office furniture has become a growing industry in itself. However, in many respects this aspect of office automation still has a long way to go. Unfortunately, the most common barrier to adequate office ergonomics is inadequate economics. Immediate production demands and a reluctance to spend adequate sums on office environment upgrades result in slow progress towards implementation of needed office improvements. As demands for better working conditions increase, however, we will see more and more offices investing in the safety and productivity of their office personnel by proper attention to the ergonomic factors we have discussed.

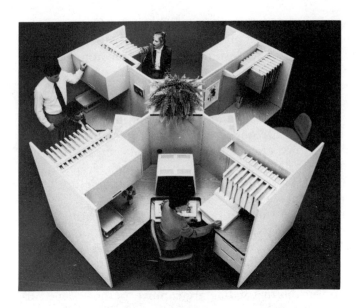

Figure 4-8. A modular design cluster workcenter. *(Photo courtesy of TAB Products Company.)*

Figure 4-9. A work station utilizing modular-style office furniture. *(Photo courtesy of Viking Acoustical Corporation.)*

To see how your office setting measures up as regards to these ergonomic factors, the following checklist is provided which gives a listing of key points to inspect.

	VERY POOR	POOR	ADEQUATE	VERY GOOD
1. Overall room lighting	_____	_____	_____	_____
2. Illumination of immediate work area	_____	_____	_____	_____
3. Control of VDT glare	_____	_____	_____	_____
4. Control of office noise level	_____	_____	_____	_____
5. Air quality/ ventilation	_____	_____	_____	_____
6. Room temperature control	_____	_____	_____	_____
7. Sufficient space at work station	_____	_____	_____	_____
8. Comfortable desk height and design	_____	_____	_____	_____
9. Comfortable chair height and design	_____	_____	_____	_____
10. General office cleanliness	_____	_____	_____	_____
11. Office organization and layout	_____	_____	_____	_____
12. Proper safety concern regarding electronic equipment, power cords, outlets, etc.	_____	_____	_____	_____
13. Scheduling work breaks	_____	_____	_____	_____

A Further Reading & Reference Guides

The Word Processing Handbook
A Short Course in Computer Literacy
Peter A. McWilliams
Prelude Press
944 North Palm Ave., Suite 10
Los Angeles, CA 90069
(1982)

The Word Processing Handbook
A Step by Step Guide to Automating Your Office
Katherine Aschner
Self-Counsel Press
Vancouver, British Columbia
Canada
(1981)

Word and Information Processing
Mary Anne Flynn
Elizabeth Walls
Reston Publishing Co., Inc.
11480 Sunset Hills Road
Reston, VA 22090
(1984)

WORD
PROCESSING
IN GENERAL

Word Processing Handbook
Ivan Flores
Van Nostrand Reinhold Co., Inc.
135 W. 50th Street
New York, NY 10020
(1983)
[540 pages, very thorough coverage & good technical data]

Understanding Computers: What Managers and Users Need To Know
Myles E. Walsh
John Wiley and Sons, Inc.
605 Third Avenue
New York, NY 10158
(1979)

WORD PROCESSING EQUIPMENT

Affordable Word Processing
Richard A. McGrath
Prentice-Hall, Inc.
Englewood Cliffs, NJ 07632
(1983)

Choosing A Word Processor
Philip I. Good
Reston Publishing Co., Inc.
11480 Sunset Hills Road
Reston, VA 22090
(1982)

How To Buy A Word Processor
Electronic Typewriters, Personal Computers, and Dedicated Systems
Steven Manus and Michael Scriven
Alfred Publishing Co., Inc.
15335 Morrison Street
P.O. Box 5964
Sherman Oaks, CA 91413
(1982)

Low Cost Word Processing
Laurence Press
Addison-Wesley Publishing Company
Jacob Way
Reading, MA 01867
(1983)

Word Processing Buyer's Guide
Arthur Naiman
BYTE/McGraw-Hill
70 Main Street
Peterborough, NH 03458
(1983)

Word Processing Using The IBM Displaywriter: Production & Applications
Rebecca C. Latif
Reston Publishing Co., Inc.
11480 Sunset Hills Road
Reston, VA 22090
(1983)

Word Processing Input
Dorinda A. Clippinger
Reston Publishing Co., Inc.
11480 Sunset Hills Road
Reston, VA 22090
(1983)

Word Processing Made Simple
Comprehensive Guide for Self Study and Review
Betty and Warner A. Hutchinson
Made Simple Books
Doubleday & Company
245 Park Avenue
New York, NY 10167
(1984)

Word Processing On Wang Systems
J. M. Williford
Wiley Press
John Wiley and Sons, Inc.
605 Third Avenue
New York, NY 10158
(1984)

Philips/Micom Word Processing Production & Applications
Rebecca C. Latif
Reston Publishing Co., Inc.
11480 Sunset Hills Road
Reston, VA 22090
(1984)

Word Processing Skills And Applications Using Wang Systems
Agnes F. Cecala
Reston Publishing Co., Inc.
11480 Sunset Hills Road
Reston, VA 22090
(1983)

Write, Edit & Print
Word Processing With Personal Computers
A Complete How-To Manual
Donald McCum
Design Enterprises of San Francisco
P.O. Box 14695
San Francisco, CA 94114

Word Processing For Executives And Professionals
Timothy R. V. Foster
Alfred Glossbrenner
Van Nostrand Reinhold Company
135 W. 50th St.
New York, NY 10020
(1983)

USERS GUIDES & MANUALS FOR WORD PROCESSING SOFTWARE

Introduction To WordStar
Arthur Naiman
Sybex, Inc.
2344 Sixth St.
Berkeley, CA 94710
(1983)

The Foolproof Guide To Scripsit Word Processing
Jeff Berner
Sybex, Inc.
2344 Sixth St.
Berkeley, CA 94710
(1983)

WordStar For The IBM PC
A Self-Guided Tutorial
Micro Workshop of Cambridge
Edwin W. Meyer
Molly E. Oldfield
David S. Wilson
Robert J. Brady Co.
Prentice-Hall Publishing Co.
Englewood Cliffs, NJ 07632
(1984)

WordStar Made Easy
Walter A. Ettlin
Osborne/McGraw-Hill
2600 Tenth Street
Berkeley, CA 94710
(1982)

TRS-80 Word Processing Applications Using Superscripsit
Carol M. Lehman
Reston Publishing Co., Inc.
11480 Sunset Hills Road
Reston, VA 22090
(1984)

Getting Started with Microsoft WORD
Janet Rampa
Microsoft Press
10700 Northup Way
Box 97200
Bellevue, WA 98009
(1984)

CP/M User's Guide
Thom Hogan
Osborne/McGraw-Hill
2600 Tenth Street
Berkeley, CA 94710
(1984)

Mastering CP/M
Alan Miller
Sybex, Inc.
2344 Sixth St.
Berkeley, CA 94710
(1983)

MS-DOS User's Guide
Paul Hoffman
Tamara Nicoloff
Osborne/McGraw-Hill
2600 Tenth Street
Berkeley, CA 94710
(1984)

Running MS-DOS
Van Wolverton
Microsoft Press
10700 Northup Way
Box 97200
Bellevue, WA 98009

The World of PC-DOS
Peter H. Mackie
Dilithium Press
P.O. Box E
Beaverton, OR 97075
(1984)

Real World UNIX
John D. Halamka
Sybex, Inc.
2344 Sixth St.
Berkeley, CA 94710
(1984)

OPERATING SYSTEMS

CAREERS IN WORD PROCESSING

Career Guide For Word Processing
Hal Cornelius and William Lewis
Monarch Press
Simon & Schuster Building
1230 Avenue of the Americas
New York, NY 10020
(1983)

Word Processing Skills And Applications
Mary Anne Flynn
Elizabeth Walls
Reston Publishing Co., Inc.
11480 Sunset Hills Road
Reston, VA 22090
(1984)

Your Future In Word Processing
Phyllis J. Peck
Gilbert J. Konkel
Richards Rosen Press, Inc.
29 E. 21st Street
New York, NY 10010
(1981)

DATA BASE

Data Base
A Primer
C. J. Date
Addison-Wesley Publishing Company
Jacob Way
Reading, MA 01867
(1983)

Database Management Systems
David Kruglinski
Osborne/McGraw-Hill
630 Bancroft Way
Berkeley, CA 94710
(1983)

Microbook: Database Management For the IBM Personal Computer
T. G. Lewis
Dilithium Press
P.O. Box E
Beaverton, OR 97075
(1983)

"OMNI" Online Database Directory
Mike Edelhart
Owen Davies
MacMillan Publishing Co.
866 Third Ave.
New York, NY 10022
(1983)

Word Processing and Business Graphics
Walter Sikonowiz
Micro-Text Publications
Prentice-Hall, Inc.
Englewood Cliffs, NJ 07632
(1982)

GRAPHICS

A Manager's Guide To Local Networks
Frank Derfler
William Stallings
Prentice-Hall, Inc.
Englewood Cliffs, NJ 07632
(1983)

LOCAL AREA NETWORKS

Computing Power For Your Law Office
Daniel Remer
SYBEX, Inc.
2344 Sixth St.
Berkeley, CA 94710
(1983)

LEGAL APPLICATIONS

The Law Office Guide To Small Computers
Forest Dean Rhoads
John Edwards
Shepard's/McGraw-Hill
Colorado Springs, CO
(1984)

Black's Law Dictionary
Henry C. Black, M.A.
West Publishing Company
50 W. Kellogg Blvd.
St. Paul, MN 55164
(1983)

REFERENCE MATERIALS—LEGAL

Law Dictionary
Steven H. Giffs
Barron's Educational Series Inc.
113 Crossways Park Drive
Woodbury, NY 11797
(1975)

Legal Secretary's Handbook
(Eleventh Edition, Calif.)
Legal Secretaries, Inc.
Parker & Son, Inc.
P.O. Box 60001
Los Angeles, CA 90060
(1977)

BUSINESS APPLICATIONS

Word Processing
A Guide For Small Business
Brian R. Smith and
Daniel J. Austin
Lewis Publishing Company
15 Muzzey St.
Lexington, MA 02173
(1983)

REFERENCE MATERIALS— BUSINESS

A Clear and Simple Guide to Business and Letter Writing
Solomon Wiener
Monarch Press
Simon & Schuster Building
1230 Avenue of the Americas
New York, NY 10020
(1983)

Complete Secretary's Handbook
Fifth Edition
Lillian Doris & Besse May Miller
rev. Mary A. DeVries
Prentice-Hall, Inc.
Englewood Clifs, NY 07632
(1983)

Modern Business Language & Usage in Dictionary Form
J. Harold Janis
Doubleday & Co., Inc.
245 Park Ave.
New York, NY 10167
(1984)

Secretarial & Administrative Procedures
Lucy Mae Jennings
Prentice-Hall, Inc.
Englewood Cliffs, NJ 07632
(1978)

Secretary's Handbook
A Manual of Correct Usage
Sarah A. Taintor
Kate M. Monro
MacMillan Pub. Co., Inc.
866 3rd Ave.
New York, NY 10022

Standard Handbook For Secretaries
Lois Hutchinson
McGraw-Hill Book Co.
1221 Avenue of the Americas
New York, NY 10020
(1979)

Webster's New World Secretarial Handbook
Simon & Schuster, Inc.
Simon & Schuster Building
1230 Avenue of the Americas
New York, NY 10020
(1981)

Webster's Secretary's Handbook
Beryl Frank
Castle Books/Books Sales Inc.
110 Enterprise Ave.
Secaucus, NJ 07094
(1980)

Word Division
Supplemental Guide to U.S. Gov't Printing Office Style Manual
Superintendent of Documents
U.S. Government Printing Office
Washington, DC 20402

Automating Your Office
James H. Green
McGraw-Hill Book Company
1221 Avenue of the Americas
New York, NY 10020

**OFFICE
AUTOMATION**

Office Automation
A Manager's Guide
Harry Katzan, Jr.
Amacon Book Division
American Management Associations
135 W. 50th Street
New York, NY 10020

PERIODICALS & OTHER PUBLICATIONS

Business Computing
The PC Magazine for Business
P.O. Box 815
Tulsa, OK 74101

[Published monthly by Penn Well Publishing Company. Executive/editorial offices at 119 Russell St., Littleton, Massachusetts 01460. Very good coverage of various microcomputer related subject areas including wp software, data bases, new hardware/software products, etc.]

Business Software
The Business Magazine for Computer Solutions
P.O. Box 27975
San Diego, CA 92128

[Published monthly by M&T Publishing, Inc., 2464 Embarcado Way, Palo Alto, California 94303. Contains very informative articles on numerous topics such as wp software, local area networks, data bases, electronic mail, etc.]

Information And Word Processing Report
The Newsletter of Information Systems.
Greyer Publications, Inc.
Madison Avenue
New York, NY 10010

[News and Technical Guidance for the professional community involved with automated business communications and related office systems. Published twice a month.]

Infosystems
The Magazine For Information Systems Management
Hitchcock Publishing Company
Hitchcock Building
Wheaton, IL 60188

[Informative articles on various topics of interest to those in information systems management. Published monthly.]

Legal Tech Newsletter
Leader Publications, Inc.
Suite 900
111 Eighth Avenue
New York, NY 10011

[A professional monthly magazine that reports developments in law office automation. Leader Publications, Inc. is affiliated with the New York Law Journal and The National Law Journal]

Modern Office Technology
1111 Chester Ave.
Cleveland, OH 44114

[Excellent coverage of various subjects such as Office Automation, Systems and Information Management, new technical developments, and others.]

Office Administration and Automation
The Operations Magazine for Administrative Systems Executives
Greyer Publications, Inc.
Madison Avenue
New York, NY 10010

[An independent business magazine published monthly. It is intended for office administrators & systems executives in every field and is not the official organ of any group or organization.]

Report to Legal Management
Altman & Weil Publications, Inc.
Haverford Road
P.O. Box 472
Ardmore, PA 19003

The Word
Office Technology Management Association
9401 W. Beloit Road
Suite 101
Milwaukee, WI 53227

[Published bi-monthly by the Office Technology Management Association (formerly the Word Processing Society) to promote an understanding of word processing and office automation within the business community.]

B

Addresses of Vendors/Services

A.B. Dick Company
5700 West Touchy
Chicago, IL 60648

A.M. Jacquard Systems
P.O. Box 604
Inglewood, CA 90312

ATEX, Inc.
32 Wiggins Ave., Dept. 192
Bedford, MA 01730

[The leading manufacturer of computerized text processing systems for publishing and publishing-like applications.)

Barrister Information Systems, Corp.
One Technology Center
46 Oak Street
Buffalo, NY 14203

C.P.T. Corporation
8100 Mitchell Road
Minneapolis, MN 90404

Datapoint Corporation
9725 Datapoint Drive
San Antonio, TX 78284

INFORMATION
PROCESSING
PRODUCTS/
SERVICES

Digital Equipment Corporation
146 Main Street
Maynard, MA 01754

EXXON Office Systems
777 Long Ridge Road
Stamford, CT 06904

Hewlett-Packard
5400 W. Rosencrans Blvd.
Lawndale, CA 90260

Honeywell Information Systems, Inc.
Office Systems Marketing
Office Management Systems Division
300 Concord Road
Billerica, MA 01821

IBM Corporation
National Marketing Center—Dept. 86R
1133 Westchester Avenue
White Plains, NY 10604

Lanier Business Systems
1700 Chautily Drive N.E.
Atlanta, GA 30324

NBI, Inc.
P.O. Box 9001
1695 38th Street
Boulder, CO 80301

Philips Information Systems, Inc.
4040 McEwen Drive
Dallas, TX 75234

Sony Product Information
P.O. Box 423
Little Falls, NJ 07424

Syntrex, Inc.
246 Industrial Way West
Eatontown, NJ 07742

Wang Laboratories, Inc.
1 Industrial Avenue
Lowell, MA 01851

Wordplex
141 Triunfo Canyon Road
Westlake Village, CA 91361

Xerox Corporation
Office Systems Division
1341 West Mockingbird Lane
Dallas, TX 75247

Burroughs Corporation
30 Main Street
Danbury, CT 06810

Compuscan, Inc.
81 Two Bridges Road, Bldg. 2
Fairfield, NJ 07006

Hendrix Incorporated
670 N. Commercial Street
Manchester, NH 03010

International Technology Corporation
6861 Elm Street
P.O. Box 772
McLean, VA 22101

TOTEC U.S.A.
19151 Parthenia Street
Suite A
Northridge, CA 91324

**OPTICAL
CHARACTER
READERS**

Anchor Automation
6624 Valjean Avenue
Van Nuys, CA 91406

Anderson Jacobson
25 Olympia Avenue
Wolburn, MA 01801

Bizcomp Corporation
P.O. Box 7498
Menlo Park, CA 94025

Cemertek Microelectronics
1308 Borregas Avenue
Sunnyvale, CA 94088-3565

Datec Modem
200 Eastowne Drive
Suite 116
Chapel Hill, NC 27514

MODEMS

Emtrol Systems Inc.
123 Locust Street
Lancaster, PA 17602

Gandolf Data Inc.
1019 South Noel Avenue
Wheeling, IL 60090

General Data Communications
One Kennedy Avenue
Danbury, CT 06810

Hayes Microcomputer
Products, Inc.
5835 Peachtree Corners East
Norcross, GA 30092

Lexicon Corporation
1541 N.W. 65th Avenue
Fort Lauderdale, FL 33313

MFJ Enterprises Inc.
921 Louisville Road
Starkville, MS 39759

Microperipheral Corporation
2643 451st Place N.E.
Redmond, WA 98052

Multi-Tech Systems Inc.
82 Second Avenue S.E.
New Brighton, MN 55112

Novation Inc.
18664 Oxnard Street
Tarzana, CA 93156

Omnitec Data
2405 South 20th Street
Phoenix, AZ 85034

Racal-Vadic
1525 McCarthy Boulevard
Milpitas, CA 95035

Rixon Inc.
120 Industrial Parkway
Silver Spring, MD 20904

Tandy Corp./Radio Shack
1500 One Tandy Center
Fort Worth, TX 76102

Tri-Data
505 E. Middlefield
Mountain View, CA 94043

Universal Data Systems
Information Systems Division
5000 Bradford Drive
Huntsville, AL 35805-1953

Amperex Electronic Corp.
Subsidiary of North America Philips
230 Duffy Avenue
Hicksville, NY 11802

Data Products
6200 Canoga Avenue
Woodland Hills, CA 91365

Datapoint Corporation
9725 Datapoint Street
San Antonio, TX 78284

Diablo Systems Incorporated
901 Page Avenue
P.O. Box 5030
Fremont, CA 94537

Digital Equipment Corporation
Continental Boulevard
Merrimack, NH 03054

Hewlett-Packard
1000 Circle Road
Corvallis, OR 97330

IBM Corporation
National Marketing Division
4111 Northside Parkway NW
Atlanta, GA 30327

NEC Information Systems
5 Militia Drive
Lexington, MA 02173

QUME Corporation
2350 Qume Drive
San Jose, CA 95131

Texas Instruments
P.O. Box 202145
Dallas, TX 75220

Wang Laboratories
One Industrial Avenue
Lowell, MA 01851

**DICTATION
EQUIPMENT**

Dictaphone Corporation
120 Old Post Road
Rye, NY 10580

Norelco Dictation Systems
Philips Business Systems
810 Woodbury Road
Woodbury, NY 11797

SONY Information Products Corporation
9 West 57th Street
New York, NY 10019

**LEGAL
MANAGEMENT
CONSULT-
ANTS**

Hildebrandt Inc.
Executive Office
182 West High Street
Somerville, NJ 08876

Cantor & Co. Inc.
Suburban Station Building
Philadelphia, PA 19103

CIP Systems, Inc.
Management & Data Processing Consultants
9460 Wilshire Boulevard
Suite 814
Beverly Hills, CA 90212

**LEGAL OFFICE
AUTOMATION/
DATA BASE
CREATION/
ETC.**

American Legal Systems
1 Embarcadero Center, Suite 2207
San Francisco, CA 94111

Aspen Systems Corp.
330 Madison Avenue
New York, NY 10017

Atlis Systems, Inc.
8460 Tyco Road
Vienna, VA 22180

Cuadra Associates
2001 Wilshire Boulevard
Suite 305
Santa Monica, CA 90403

Digital Business Center
15436 Ventura Boulevard
Sherman Oaks, CA 91403

Directory of Online Databases
Cuadra Associates, Inc.
2001 Wilshire Boulevard
Suite 305
Santa Monica, CA 90403

Endata
421 Great Circle Road
Nashville, TN 37228

Equitrac Corporation
3200 Ponce De Leon Boulevard
Coral Gables, FL 33134

Guardian Automated Systems
600 Liberty Bank Building
420 Main Street
Buffalo, NY 14202

Information Consultants, Inc.
2021 L Street, N.W.
Suite 300
Washington, DC 20036

Alpine Data Systems
2040 Avenue of the Stars
Suite 400
Los Angeles, CA 90027

Barrister Information Systems Corporation
45 Oak Street
Buffalo, NY 14203

CIP Systems, Inc.
9460 Wilshire Boulevard
Suite 814
Beverly Hills, CA 90212

Compulaw
3520 Wesley Street
Culver City, CA 90230

Cybernetics Resource Corporation
10 Maple Street
Port Washington, NY 11050

LEGAL OFFICE ACCOUNTING/ FINANCIAL MANAGE- MENT

Danyl Corporation
1509 Glen Avenue
Morrestown, NJ 08057

Data Law Company
6341 S. Troy Circle
Suite E
Englewood, CO 80111

Elite Communication Systems
7515 Beverly Blvd.
Los Angeles, CA 90036

Guardian Automated Systems
600 Liberty Bank Building
420 Main Street
Buffalo, NY 14202

O A Software Inc.
2185 The Alameda
San Jose, CA 95126

Tritek Data Corporation
6263 Variel Avenue
Woodland Hills, CA 91367

SOFTWARE FOR LEGAL APPLICATIONS

Aspen Systems Corporation
330 Madison Avenue
New York, NY 10017
   [litigation support; data bases; & more]

Attorneys Software, Inc.
P.O. Box 1408
Covina, CA 91722
   [law practice management, billings etc.]

Compulaw, Inc.
3520 Wesley Street
Culver City, CA 90230
   [client management software]

Data Law Company
6341 South Troy Circle
Suite E
Englewood, CA 80111
   [litigation support; law practice management]

D-2 Software Systems
3857 Birch Street
Suite 285
Newport Beach, CA 92660
   [docket and calendaring system]

Informatics General Corporation
6011 Executive Boulevard
Rockville, MD 20852
  [information management systems]

Lawyers Technology Incorporated
339 15th Street
Suite 200
Oakland, CA 94612

Matthew Bender
235 East 45th Street
New York, NY 10017
  [legal systems software designed for both microcomputers and word processors]

O A Software, Inc.
2185 The Alameda
San Jose, CA 95126
  [litigation management & support; general ledger; accounting]

Plex Systems, Inc.
2900 Bristol Street
Building C
Suite 107
Costa Mesa, CA 92626
  [case management, client billings]

Satori Software
5507 Woodlawn Avenue North
Seattle, WA 98103
  [legal billing software]

LEXIS—Computer Assisted Legal Information Retrieval

NEXIS—Computer Assisted News and Information Retrieval

Meade Data Central
200 Park Avenue
New York, NY 10016

Westlaw—Computer Assisted Information Retrieval
West Publishing Co.
50 W. Kellogg Blvd.
St. Paul, MN 55164

LEGAL: COMPUTER ASSISTED RESEARCH

COMPUTER-
IZED LEGAL
RESEARCH/
WORD PRO-
CESSING
INTERFAC-
ING

Lee Technology, Inc.
327 Filbert Steps
San Francisco, CA 94133

[Applewriter IIc® (word processing software)—

Westlaw® (computerized legal research) interfacing]

Apple is a registered trademark of Apple Computer Corp. Westlaw is a registered trademark of West Publishing Company.

PC-MAIN-
FRAME INTER-
FACING

CXI, Inc.
3606 West Bayshore Road
Palo Alto, CA 94303

Oxford Software Corporation
174 Boulevard
Hasbrouck Heights, NJ 07604

WORD
PROCESSING/
COMPUTER
ACCESSORIES
& SUPPLIES

Data and Information Supplies Catalog (IBM)
International Business Machines Corporation
One Culver Road
Dayton, NJ 08810

Devoke Data Products
Devoke Company
1500 Martin Avenue
Santa Clara, CA 95050
    Furniture & Accessories
    Media & Supplies
    Cables and Interconnects
    Protection Products
    Paper Handling Products for Information processing

Global Computer Supplies
A Division of Global Computer Company
9138 Hemlock Drive
Hempstead, NY 11550
    and
20310-38 Wilmington Avenue
Compton, CA 90220
    PC Accessories
    Storage media
    Data Communication Equipment
    Ergonomic Furniture
    Supplies

Visible Computer Supply Corporation
A Subsidiary of Wallace Computer Services, Inc.
1615 S. Stockton Street
Lodi, CA 95241
　　Word processing and computer supplies and accessories

MISCO Inc.
P.O. Box 399 A6
Holmdel, NJ 07733
　　Catalog of Word Processing Supplies and Accessories

Good People
Office Automation Temporaries
41 East 42nd Street
New York, NY 10017

Kelly Services, Inc.
GPO 1179
Detroit, MI 48266

Manpower Temporary Services
(See your local phone directory)

Olsten Temporary Services
Office Automation Division
1 Merrick Avenue
Westbury, NY 11590

Word Processors Personnel Service (WPPS)
233 N. Michigan Avenue
Chicago, IL 4929
Wilshire Boulevard
Los Angeles, CA

WORD PROCESSING TEMP AGENCIES AND PLACEMENT SERVICES

Datapoint Corporation
9725 Datapoint Drive, 1-47
San Antonio, TX 78284

LOCAL AREA NETWORKS

Display Systems Leasing, Inc.
22 Second Street
San Francisco, CA 94105

[IBM Displaywriters, IBM 6670s and others]

COMPUTER/ WORD PROCESSING EQUIPMENT BROKERS/ LEASING COMPANIES

Electronic Office Exchange, Inc.
The Pre-Owned Wang Equipment People
1250 N. Main Street
P.O. Box 7337
Ann Arbor, MI 48107
(1-800-321-2986)

Erst International Corporation
225 Lafayette Street
New York, NY 10012
(1-800-FOR-ERST)

[WANG WP terminals and printers]

J. J. Bender & Associates
2357 Black Rock Turnpike
Fairfield, CT 06430
(1-800-FOR-WORD)

Target Systems Exchange
1777 Borel Place
Suite 500
San Mateo, CA 94402
(1-800-227-5071)

Word Processing Brokerage Corporation
R.D. #1 Box 190
Kempton, PA 19529
(1-800-223-9264)

WORD/ INFORMA- TION PRO- CESSING ORGANIZA- TIONS

The following list gives some of the many organizations that are active in various aspects of the information processing field. Most of these groups offer memberships of one type or another as well as informative publications.

American Federation of Information Processing Societies (AFIPS)
1899 Preston White Drive
Reston, VA 22091
(703) 620-8900

Associated Information Managers
1776 E. Jefferson Street
Suite 470S
Rockville, MD 20852
(301) 231-7447

Association of Information Systems Professionals (AISP)
1015 N. York Road
Willow Grove, PA 19090
(215) 657-3220

Data Processing Management Association (DPMA)
505 Busse Highway
Park Ridge, IL 60068
(312) 825-8124

Office Technology Management Association, Inc. (OTMA)
(formerly the International Word Processing Society)
9401 W. Beloit Road
Suite 101
Milwaukee, WI 53227
(414) 321-0880

Society of Office Automation Professionals
N. Dean Meyer, President
233 Mountain Road
Ridgefield, CT 06877
(203) 431-0029

National Institute for Occupational Safety and Health (NIOSH)
Parklawn Building
5600 Fishers Lane
Rockville, MD 20857

OCCUPA-TIONAL SAFETY GROUPS

NIOSH offers reports of research into various aspects of occupational health problems such as VDT hazzards, etc.

Occupational Safety and Health Administration (OSHA)
U. S. Department of Labor
200 Constitution Avenue N.W.
Washington, DC 20210

Safeware™
The Computer Insurance
P.O. Box 02211
Columbus, OH 43202

WORD PROCESSNG EQUIPMENT INSURANCE

Association of Computer Users (ACU)
P.O. Box 9003
Boulder, CO 80301

Viking Acoustical Corporation
Airlake Industrial Park
Lakeville, MN 55044

ERGONOMIC FURNITURE

TAB Products Company
1400 Page Mill Road
P.O. Box 10269
Palo Alto, CA 94304

C Glossary of Word/ Information Processing Terms

Abort: A term meaning to cancel, stop or end a particular function or routine. The operator may abort a procedure before it is completed or the system may be programmed to automatically abort a procedure when certain conditions are reached or not reached.

Access Time: (1) The amount of time that elapses between the calling for information electronically and the time at which it becomes available. (2) The length of time it takes a terminal to respond to the commands of the operator.

Acoustic Coupler: A device connected to the headset of a telephone which, in conjunction with a modem, allows computers and electronic devices to communicate with each other over phone lines. The accoustic coupler has cradle-like cups into which the telephone headset fits so that audio signals can be passed through the ear and/or mouthpiece of the phone. (See also MODEM).

Alphanumeric: A character type which can be either alphabetic or numeric, for example, 1, 4, 5, R, F, H, O. Alphanumeric can also be used to describe a string of characters or a data set which contains alphabetic or numeric characters or both, e.g., R45TH, 556#33, and 99991AB are each considered alphanumeric.

Applications Software/Applications Program: A program written with a particular application in mind, e.g., a word processing program is a particular type of application program. A cost accounting program would be another type of application program.

Archive/Archiving: (1) Archive is a function of many word processors whereby information on a diskette is protected from accidental erasure or simply preserved in its original format. (2) Archiving also means to make a copy of information and store it on an auxiliary storage medium for later use.

ASCII (pronounced "Askee"): *A*merican *S*tandard *C*ode for *I*nformation *I*nterchange. A symbolic code used to represent characters or bits of information in a computer system. Computer systems communicate with one another via such symbolic codes. Most non-IBM systems use ASCII. IBM systems usually use an internal code referred to as EBCDIC, but communication links can be set up which allow use of ASCII.

Asynchronous Communication: A type of information transmission where each character of information is surrounded by one or more start and stop bits which indicate the starting and ending points of the information. In asynchronous communication, the data is sent as soon as it is ready rather than being sent at specific intervals.

Background Printing: A WP system option that allows for the printing of a document while the keyboard and screen are left operational for performing other tasks.

Backup: A duplicate copy of a document or a whole diskette as a safeguard in the event of accidental loss or erasure of the original data.

Baud: A unit of measurement of speed of transmission between a computer/word processor and a peripheral device or another terminal.

Baud Rate: A unit of measurement of speed of transmission from one device to another, e.g., from a WP terminal to a printer or from an OCR device to a WP terminal. A baud rate of 9600, for example, indicates that approximately 9600 bits per second of information are being transmitted from the sending to the receiving device. This 9600 bits per second (or bps) is roughly equivalent to 960 words per minute.

Bidirectional Printing: A technique of printing employed by many daisy wheel and other printers where one line of text is printed as the print wheel moves from left to right and the next line immediately following is printed as the print wheel moves from right to left. Bidirectional printing avoids unnecessary typing carriage movement and thus saves time.

Binary: A numbering system which is based on **two** rather than based on **ten** as is the common decimal system. The binary system, which uses only the digits zero (0) and one (1), is ideally suited to computer operations since zero and one can be represented internally by a plus or minus value or an *on* or *off* condition.

Bit (Binary Digit): The smallest unit of information that can be stored in a computer system. A group of eight bits taken together is called a Byte.

Bit Rate: The rate at which binary digits are transmitted over a communications channel. Often expressed as bits per second (bps). Sometimes used interchangeably with baud rate. (See Baud Rate.)

Boilerplate: (1) Text that is standardized or used very often in more than one application. (2) Standardized text stored on a WP system for repeated use.

Buffer: A part of memory used to store information temporarily while some other function is being executed. Information transmitted from one machine to another is often received into a buffer first, to prevent loss of information sent faster than the receiving machine can utilize it.

Byte: A group of bits read together as a single unit. A byte usually contains eight bits. A byte represents one character of data. For example, the character "A" would be stored in memory as one single byte. Memory and storage areas are measured in terms of byte capacity, e.g., kilobytes (1Kb = 1,024 bytes) or megabytes (1Mb = 1,048,576).

CE: Customer Engineer.

CRT (Cathode Ray Tube): Refers to the display screen of a WP terminal. A CRT is a vacuum tube which focuses an internal electron beam onto a luminescent screen to produce visible images. A CRT works on similar principles as a TV screen.

CPU (Central Processing Unit): The central part of a computer which actually does the computing as distinguished from the peripheral devices which are used for input, output and storage. The CPU contains three main elements: (1) the Arithmetic Logic Unit (ALU) which carries out high-speed arithmetic calculations and logical comparisons; (2) the control unit which controls the operation of the system as a whole; and (3) the main memory unit (also called central storage or main storage).

Computer Graphics: Graphs, tables, charts, or drawings generated by a computer and displayed on a VDT or output on a printer.

Copy Holder: A tray or stand for holding text for easy reading by a WP terminal operator.

CP/M (Control Program for Microcomputers): An operating system for microcomputers. CP/M is in widespread use throughout the office automation environment and there are now thousands of CP/M based software packages available for various applications such as word processing, billings, accounting, etc. CP/M is a registered trademark of Digital Research, Inc.

CPS (Characters per second): Usually refers to the rate of speed of a printer or similar device.

Crash: A major system failure due to hardware or software malfunction or operator error. A "crashed" system can be very costly in terms of time and loss of data. (See also Head Crash.)

Cursor: A character or symbol, such as a block or underscore, on a video display terminal that indicates where the next character is going to appear or where the next action is to be taken. WP terminals often vary from one another in how the cursor appears and how it is moved about on the screen.

Daisy Wheel: A printing element shaped like a wheel with printing characters around its circumference. The daisy wheel is usually used in letter quality printers since it is capable of producing high quality type. Daisy wheel printers are one of the many types of impact printers available.

Data Base: A specifically designed and organized file which can be accessed by a number of different users for different purposes. A data base file is usually organized so that information records can be quickly accessed by the use of keywords or subject headings. A data base is a centralized body of data which can be shared by various terminals which have different data requirements. The overall size and organization of a data base varies with the type of organization it is designed to service.

Data Processing: (1) Very broadly, data processing means the manipulation and organization of data into specific arrangements for a particular use, whether done manually, electronically, or both. (2) More narrowly, data processing refers to the input, manipulation, storage and access of numerical and/or statistical data through the use of computer systems. Under this more narrow definition, data processing is distinguished from word processing in that it focuses on the processing of numerical data rather than text.

Dedicated System/Dedicated Word Processor: A computer system or device designed for a particular application. A word processing system that is mainly designed for word processing work is said to be a *dedicated system*. A dedicated word processor is sometimes abbreviated as DWP.

Density: The amount of information stored per unit area of a particular storage device.

Disk (aka Hard Disk):   A magnetic storage device capable of storing millions of characters of data. Information on a disk can be stored in various areas called cylinders or smaller areas called tracks. Stored data is accessed by read/write heads which locate the particular track or cylinder on which the needed data is stored. Storage capacity of hard disks is usually measured in megabytes. A 2.5 megabyte disk, for example, is capable of storing 2,500,000 characters of data, or over 1,000 pages of text.

DOS (Disk Operating System):   An operating system that uses disks for its auxiliary storage rather than magnetic tape or other storage media. (See operating system.)

Display: In word processing, display usually refers to the output shown on the screen of a CRT terminal.

Dot Matrix: (1) A grid on which a series of dots are plotted to form a particular character. (2) A dot matrix printer is one which prints characters formed by a combination of tiny dots. Dot matrix printers are commonly used for high speed printing (e.g., 200 cps and up) but are not as well suited to high quality printing as are impact printers.

Down Time: Refers to the time during which a computer system is not operating due to some malfunction, power failure or repair operation.

Dumb Terminal: A "dumb" terminal is one that does not have a microprocessor and must rely on a separate central processing unit in order to perform any high level tasks.

DWP: See Dedicated Word Processor.

Editrace: A WP option which allows the changes or revision from a previous draft to show on a printout which changes can then be retained or reversed.

Electronic Mail: Instantaneous transmission of text from one terminal over phone lines to a terminal at a different location, or over direct cable connections to another terminal in the same office of building. The text can then be stored by the second terminal or output on its printer. Electronic mail is a form of telecommunications.

Embedded Command: Special command words placed into the text in a word processor which are instructions to the WP system and not printed as part of the text. An example of an imbedded command would be a series of symbols such as "$$@" placed at the end of a line instructing the word processor to advance to the next page when it reaches this point.

EOF: End of file.

EOF Marker: A marker or symbol that indicates that the end of a particular file has been reached.

EOT: Abbreviation for "End of Transmission."

Ergonomics: The science of human engineering which deals with the interaction of people with the mechanics of technical equipment and the overall working environment in order to determine the optimum design and arrangement of equipment for comfort, ease of operation and productivity. Sometimes called "human factors" or "biotechnology."

Execution Time: (1) The time it takes to carry out a particular instruction or procedure. (2) That portion of an instruction cycle during which a procedure is performed or a program is executed.

Fan Fold Paper: Paper designed for continuous feed into a printer by use of a tractor feed device. The paper is in long continuous sheets, perforated and folded at page intervals and has perforated edges with holes to fit the tractor feed device. Sometimes called Z-fold or tractor paper.

Field: (1) An area of storage within a record. The common terminology for storage hierarchy in ascending order of size is *field, record, file, data base.* (2) A group of characters (or one character) which mean something (e.g., "M" (male) or "F" (female)).

File: (1) A group of records assembled for a particular purpose. (2) File records are usually related to each other in some way, such as by subject matter, but can be simply stored by quantity.

Flag: An indicator at a particular location in the software or hardware which points out or indicates when particular condition or location has been reached.

Floppy Disk: A flexible circular magnetic disk, usually made of mylar, on which data can be stored. Used in the disk drive of a WP or computer terminal, the disk rotates as electronic read/write heads and stores or retrieves information from the disk. A floppy disk provides random access storage of data.

Font: A term designating a particular style of type.

Format: The precise layout of a document. The basic elements of the format are paper size, line spacing, margins, and typeface, and can include any specialized arrangement of the text as may be required by the user, such as headings, bold typefacing, and indentations.

Full Duplex: In electronic communications, full duplex means the simultaneous communication in both directions between two electronic devices.

Global Search: An option in WP software that allows the operator to set up an automatic search throughout a document or file for a particular word, title, phrase, character or number. Variations on global search are used to check for every occurrence of a word, to check for and replace one term with another throughout a document, and to go to a particular location in a document or file where a name or title is mentioned.

GPM   (General   Purpose   Microcomputer): Usually   refers   to   a microcomputer used for general business applications which may include word processing as well as other tasks.

Graphics: (1) Symbols, shapes, lines, bars, etc. used in constructing charts and graphs for visual illustrations of statistical information. Graphic data can be output on either video display terminals or printers if such are equipped to handle the graphics option. (2) The term graphics is also used to describe the software capability itself.

Half Duplex: A system capable of transmitting in either of two directions but not in both directions simultaneously.

Hard Copy: Output in a permanent form, e.g., paper, rather than on video display terminals. Sometimes referred to simply as "copy."

Hard Disk: A magnetic storage medium consisting of magnetically coated plastic on which characters of information can be stored. Hard disks are larger, more expensive and capable of holding more information than floppy disks or diskettes. Hard disks, often called simply "disks," are used widely in computer storage and for larger WP systems. Information retrieval from a hard disk is usually faster and more reliable than when using floppy disks.

Hardware: The actual physical components of a computer/WP system as distinguished from its software or program logic.

Hardwired: A program or series of instructions that are built into a system by the manufacturer and are unalterable by the operator.

Head: An extremely sensitive electromagnet capable of "reading" magnetized areas on magnetic storage media and "writing" data back onto storage. Sometimes referred to as "read/write" heads.

Head Crash: In disk systems, the accidental contact of the read/write heads with the surface of the disk causing damage to the disk and/or the read/write heads, and very often accompanied by a loss of data. (See also Crash.)

Image Printer: A device capable of outputting hundreds of pages of information per minute utilizing a photocopy technique rather than conventional impact printing.

Impact Printer: Printers utilizing a striking mechanism and a carbon ribbon such as daisy wheel, chain, ball, and drum printers. Impact printers are used to obtain high quality printed output such as that required for business letters, legal documents, etc.

Information Processing: A term encompassing both word processing and data processing. (See Word Processing and Data Processing in this Glossary as well as in Chapter 1.)

Ink-Jet Printer: A printer that "sprays" electrostatically charged particles of ink onto the paper in the form of various characters. Ink-jet printers can be very fast, e.g., 100 cps, but are not suited for letter quality output. Ink-jet printers are also quieter than impact printers. Some ink jet printers have multicolor capability.

I/O: Refers to the input and output devices of a WP system. Input devices include keyboard, OCR reader and modems (for long distance or conversion input from other systems). Output devices include the terminal screen, modems, and printers.

Intelligent Terminals: A video terminal and keyboard which has its own microprocessor and thus has internal processing capabilities. This is in contrast with a "dumb" terminal which does not have its own microprocessor and must rely on an outside processing unit.

Integrated Data Processing: The concept of having all systems within a business organization viewed as subsystems of a larger system which encompasses all data processing requirements within that organization. Such integration can be useful in eliminating unwanted duplication of functions and can cut down on the number of separate data entry points required.

Interface: (1) To connect a central processing unit to one or more peripheral devices. (2) (Generally) To connect two or more components of a computer/WP system in such a way that they can communicate with each other. (3) The name given to the hardware or software necessary to accomplish such linking.

ISAM (Indexed Sequential Access Method): A method of storing and retrieving data in a sequential form by use of an index. In a file set up along ISAM procedures, each record can be retrieved in sequence through the use of a "key" such as client name, by which it can be accessed. A set of indexes is maintained which keeps track of where the records are on the storage disk.

Interword Spacing: The adding of extra spaces between words in order to produce a justified text.

Interface: (noun) The point at which two systems (terminals/devices) are linked together. A connection terminal for electronic equipment which allows them to communicate electronically with one another. One of the most common electronic interface connectors is called RS-232, which has more or less become an industry standard and which is often used to connect WP terminals with printers and other peripheral devices. (verb) To connect various terminals or devices to one another to create or expand a WP or computer system.

Justify/Justification: The automatic squaring off of text at the margins to produce an even block appearance of the text such as that used in a book. In justification, the system automatically adjusts the amount of space allowed between words so as to fill out each line. Most good WP systems have the text justification option.

K (Kilobyte): A measure of memory or storage capacity. One kilobyte equals 1,024 bytes or 8,192 bits. Also abbreviated "Kb."

Key: A field containing a number, symbol or character which acts as an identifier to a particular record. A zip code could be chosen as the "key," for example, and files could then be sorted by ascending or descending zip code key.

Keyboard: The typewriter-like board of a word processing terminal used to input data, edit text, or control some operation of the system.

Laser Printer: A printer using a low-power laser to create images (characters) on the drum of a photocopier to produce printed output at a very rapid rate. Some laser printers can output text at the rate of 1800 cps or more.

Letter Quality Printer: A printer that produces high quality character output suitable for business letters, legal briefs, contracts, etc. as opposed to draft quality printers. Letter quality printers usually use a daisy wheel, ball element, or thimble element in creating typed characters.

Mag Card: (1) A magnetic card used to store text in a word processing system. (2) Sometimes used to refer to the word processing equipment itself which used such magnetic cards, such as an IBM MAG CARD II word processor.

Management Information System (MIS): An information processing system containing information on such areas as inventory, sales, payroll, accounts payable, and accounts receivable. Such information could be processed for day-to-day use by various departments within an organization, but also could readily provide management with current data as to the status of these various areas for review and evaluation.

Main Memory: The internal, immediate-access storage area of the computer as distinguished from auxiliary storage areas or devices. Also known as main store.

Math Pack, Math Package: A software option available on some word processing systems that allows the terminal to be used for arithmetic operations such as addition, subtraction, multiplication, and division.

Megabyte: A measure of storage capacity exceeding one million bytes. One megabyte equals 1024 Kilobytes.

Memory Typewriter: An electronic typewriter with an internal memory capable of temporarily storing text for automatic playback. Some memory typewriters can store three to five pages or more of text. A memory typewriter is more versatile than a standard electric typewriter but does not have the advanced capabilities of an actual word processing system.

Menu: A displayed list of functions which a word processor is capable of performing, allowing the operator the option of choosing the most appropriate function. Some typical menu functions are:

1. Create New Document
2. Rename Document File

3. Copy Document

4. Print Continuous

5. Global Search and Replace

6. Global Search and Stop

7. Reformat a File

Merge: To bring together characters, words, sentences, paragraphs, or documents into consecutive alignment.

Microprocessor: The smallest unit in a microcomputer or word processor that is actually capable of performing logical operations. A microprocessor is often just a tiny computer chip which has processing capabilities. A microcomputer or word processor must contain at least one microprocessor but can contain many.

Microcomputer: Usually refers to the smallest class of computers, such as home computers. The IBM PC, IBM PC Jr., RADIO SHACK TRS-80, and APPLE II are examples of microcomputers.

Minicomputers: Usually refers to the computers in the class between microcomputers and mainframes. Minicomputers are in between the microcomputers and the large mainframes in both computing power and price.

Mini-Disk: Also called a diskette, mini-disk refers to a floppy disk in a 5¼ inch square protective jacket.

Modem: A telecommunications device used to transmit data over the phone lines. A modem is used to convert the digital signals of a computer into analog (audio) signals which can be carried over telephone lines to another modem where they are then reconverted back into digital signals. Modem stands for *Mod*ulate-*dem*odulate. Using modems, computer systems, or word processing systems can communicate with each other or with peripheral equipment over long distances.

Motherboard: A part of computer hardware. The main circuit board in a computer into which other circuit boards are plugged or connected.

Multiplexing: Simultaneous transmission of several messages over a single communication line. In multiplexing, numerous signals are transmitted at different frequencies so that each message retains its integrity.

Multiplexor: A hardware device that allows a computer system to utilize many communication channels at once. (See Multiplexing.)

Network: A special configuration of word processing equipment, i.e., input terminals, video screens, storage devices, printers, etc., that is designed to handle a particular user demand. A network can be set up to include a large number of data input terminals and a single main processor and storage device or terminals with independent processing capabilities linked together for exchange of information. A network can be a very small, one-room arrangement of a WP system or can extend out beyond a single office to include remote terminals and peripherals in other areas.

Non-Volatile Memory: An area of memory that can retain information even after the power has been turned off.

OCR (Optical Character Reader, Optical Character Recognition):   A device capable of reading printed information and converting it into electronic signals for transmitting to a word processing terminal or other computer device. Some OCR devices require that the text be typed with a special typing element, others can read a variety of different type styles. Using an OCR device, valuable word processing time does not have to be consumed in inputting raw data into the WP system. Instead, data is simply typed on a standard typewriter and fed into the OCR scanner and immediately into the WP storage system for later editing and output. Some OCR devices are capable of reading handwritten characters as well as typed material.

Operator: One who operates or controls the functions of a word processing system directly. An operator's true skills go far beyond a knowledge of the operation of the terminal itself and includes a working knowledge of grammar, punctuation, spelling, as well as the demands of the immediate working environment and how his system interacts with other systems whether human users or other office automation equipment. The operator is the vital human link between the high technology systems and the actual end product being produced.

Overprint: To print words or characters two or more times in the same space to give a boldface effect.

Pagination: The capability of a word processing system to divide documents into contiguous segments or pages.

Parallel Transmission: A type of transmission of information where all elements of the data are transmitted simultaneously, over separate paths. Parallel transmission is faster than serial transmission. (See Serial Transmission.)

PC (Personal Computer):   A microcomputer for home or small business use.

Peripheral: An auxiliary device to the central control terminal of a word processor which has a particular function in the operation of the system as a whole. Printers, disk storage, OCR devices, and other input or display terminals are some examples of peripherals.

Pitch: In printing or video display, the number of characters per inch. Ten pitch is 10 characters per inch; 12 pitch is 12 twelve characters per inch.

Platen: The hard backing surface against which a printing mechanism strikes in order to produce a typed character, e.g. the roll of a typewriter.

Port: (1) An input or output terminal on a word processing device where cables or plugs are connected to transmit or receive information or power to or from other units. (2) A male or female connector consisting of a number of pins which fit together and are used to carry electronic signals. A common type of interfacing used to connect the ports of various devices is the RS-232 communications cable. In addition to the ports and connectors being physically compatible, the software must be capable of correctly interpreting the signals being transmitted over the communication lines.

Priority:　The order of seniority according to which work products are handled in a word processing department as determined by the specific guidelines established for that particular working environment. Ideally, priorities would be set by supervisory personnel based on actual user need, production demands and actual urgency.

Program:　(1) A set of specific instructions designed to direct a computer in performing a particular set of activities to achieve a certain result. A program may be designed to monitor other programs or simply be designed for one particular application. (2) The software or logic which indicates how the input data is to be processed. (See Software).

Prompt:　A software generated message appearing on the screen of a display terminal which gives information to the operator such as an indication that a particular condition has been reached or request that the operator execute a particular command.

Proofread:　Reading text for the purpose of locating and indicating errors so that they may be corrected. Such errors searched for include mistakes in spelling, grammar, typing, OCR misreads, printing, context, spacing, and format.

Printwheel:　A wheel-shaped printing mechanism, usually about three inches in diameter, that has alphabetic and numeric characters on stems around its circumference and is used to produce letter quality output. A printwheel, also called a daisy wheel, is most effective for speeds ranging from 35 CPS to 65 CPS.

Queue:　A number of items lined up consecutively for processing, inputting or outputting.

Qwerty Keyboard:　The name given to the standard keyboard used on most typewriters, word processors, and microcomputers. Word processors and microcomputers will also have special functions keys in addition to the standard Qwerty keys.

RAM (Random Access Memory):　A type of memory in which data is directly accessible by the central processing unit regardless of the memory location in which the data is located. Data can be read into and read from RAM very rapidly.

Raw Input:　Written text that has to be manually typed for input into OCR or directly through a word processing terminal.

Repeat Key:　(1) A key on a word processor keyboard that when held down has a repeating function. The space bar, period, and underline keys are usually repeat keys. (2) A special key that when pressed in conjunction with another key causes the second key to have a repeating function.

Retrieve:　To call back data from storage so that it can be used.

Reverse Video:　An option on some word processing display terminals that allows the characters to be displayed as dark against a light background instead of the more commonly used light characters against a dark background.

ROM (Read Only Memory):　A type of memory that is fixed and cannot be added to or changed only "read from."

RS-232: A standard 25-pin connector for word processing and computer terminals which allows interfacing with other electronic devices.

Scroll: To move text past the viewing window of a WP screen to display the portion of the document needed.

Screen: The visual display output unit of a computer or word processing terminal.

Search: An option on many word processors that allows the system to automatically search an entire document for a particular character, symbol, word, or phrase. Variations of the search option include Search and Stop, i.e., the search process stops at the point where the item being searched for is found; and Search and Replace, where the system can be instructed by the operator to search for one item of data and replace it with another item of data.

Sequential: Sequential refers to a method of storage where the elements of data are stored in sequence, one after the other. Accessing a sequential data file is slower than random access. Magnetic tapes reels or cassettes are examples of sequential data storage media.

Serial: In series (see Sequential).

Serial Transmission: A type of transmission where data bits are sent one after the other, in sequence.

Shared Logic: A system whereby several operating terminals can share the same central processing unit and main storage.

Smart Terminal: A terminal that has its own microprocessor and can perform some operations independently from a large host system. Sometimes called an intelligent terminal.

Software: (1) The programs or instructions that direct the operations of a computer system. Software is a general term that can be applied to a particular program or to a collection of programs. Whole software "packages" can be designed for a particular application such as accounting, inventory management, production control, or word processing. (Contrast with Hardware.) (2) The term "software" has at times been expanded to include training manuals, and other administrative tools of the operator, but more commonly it refers to the actual programs themselves.

Speller: A software option in many word processors which compares the text of a document to an internal dictionary of thousands of words and notifies the operator of possible misspelled words within the text. (Also referred to as Spelling Checker, Dictionary, and Word Search).

Split Screen: A word processing display terminal option allowing the operator to view parts of two or more different documents or parts of documents simultaneously. Split screen functions can be used for cross checking information, or for copying from one document to another.

Spooling: The procedure of temporarily storing data on disks or magnetic tape until it is ready for processing or printing.

Standalone: A word processing terminal capable of "standing alone," i.e., a terminal capable of operating independently from another terminal or central processing unit.

State-of-the-Art: The highest level of technical quality available for general use in a particular application.

Station: (1) An arrangement of the components necessary to establish a single, working word processing installation. For example, a station might consist of a video terminal and keyboard, a printer and disk drives. (2) The whole work area assigned to a single word processing specialist, consisting of wp terminal, printer, disk drives, desk, chair, paper supplies and all needed reference materials.

Stop Code: A character inserted in the text by an operator which causes a printer to stop printing when it reaches that point.

Storage: Specific areas of space allocated on a storage medium for the holding of information until it is needed.

Storage Media: Devices capable of storing or saving information for later use. Internal memory, floppy disks, diskettes, hard disks, magnetic cards, and magnetic tape are examples of storage media.

Subroutine: A series of logical steps in a program which perform a particular task or calculation and which can be called or used repeatedly by the main program.

Subscript: A function key that allows a character to be printed slightly lower on the print line than the other characters.

Superscript: A function key that allows a character to be printed slightly higher on the print line than the other characters.

Surge: A sudden increase of power in an electrical circuit which can cause errors or difficulties in the operation of a computer or word processing system. Surge protection devices are generally available to protect electronic terminals against damage from power surges.

Systems Software: Programs that control the overall operations of a system or the interaction of other programs within a system. Systems software is usually supplied by the hardware manufacturer and used to coordinate the use by the system of applications software.

Telecommunications: The transmission of information electronically via telephone, satellite, cables, television or radio.

Teleprinter: A typewriter-like device capable of transmitting and receiving data to/from another terminal over a communications line.

Timesharing: A term used to describe an operation of some large computer or word processing system where the central processing unit shares its time with a number of different users, switching from one to another at very high speeds.

Tractor Feed: A mechanical attachment to a printer that allows the use of lengthy sheets of paper for continuous printing. The tractor feed device has pins on either side into which the holes in tractor paper fit and are guided along by the tractor mechanism.

Turnaround Time: The amount of time between the submission of a task to word processing and the time the product is completed.

Underscore: To underline.

Utility Program: A program designed to perform a particular operation such as formatting files, copying files, sorting, adding or deleting labels to files in storage, updating, etc. Utility programs are usually stored on separate disks and called or used only when needed.

User: The individual or group for whom a particular type of output is produced or for whom a particular problem is being solved.

User Friendly: A term describing equipment the function of which is easily grasped and is not overly technical in its day-to-day operation.

VDT (Video Display Terminal):   A word processing terminal with a visual display screen. A VDT consists of a terminal, keyboard, and CRT.

Virtual Storage: An efficient use of the physical storage capacities of a computer system in such a way as to give the functional appearance of more memory storage being available in the system than is actually present. Virtual storage operates by keeping segments of data being used in current processing in main store and calling in new segments of data as needed while transferring inactive segments from main storage to auxiliary storage to make room as needed.

Work Station: (See station).

Word Processing: (1) The input, manipulation, storage, retrieval and output of text. (2) The use by trained operators of specially designed computerized equipment to produce high quality written communication with both speed and accuracy.

Wraparound: The capability of a word processing system to automatically string words of a sentence together correctly while data is being input even when the end of a line is reached, similar to the way an automatic carriage return operates on a standard electric typewriter.

D

Glossary of Basic
Legal Terms

(Here follows a brief listing of some key legal terms and their definitions. Some legal terms have widely different meanings depending on their use in the context in which they appear. For more detailed definitions of these and other legal terms, consult one of the legal dictionaries listed in Appendix A).

Affidavit: A voluntary declaration or statement of facts made in writing and confirmed by the oath or affirmation of the party making it. An affidavit is taken before a person who has the authority to administer such oaths or affirmations.

Appeal: A plea to a higher court to review a decision of a lower court or administrative agency.

Attorney: (Generally) One who is appointed and authorized to act on behalf of another. (Specific) Attorney at Law. One who is admitted to practice law in his respective state and who is authorized to handle civil and criminal matters for his clients including the drafting of legal documents, giving of legal advice and appearing on behalf of his clients before courts and other judicial bodies.

Authority: A statute, law, legal decision, treatise, etc. that has some weight and significance in terms of making other judicial determinations. A decision in one lawsuit, for example, may be referred to in a later lawsuit involving a similar issue to show how a court of law has already approached and handled that particular issue. "Authorities" usually refers to a list of statutes, decisions, etc. in a legal pleading that the author is relying on to support his position.

Bar: (1) All attorneys, or members of the legal profession taken collectively. (2) The full court of judges sitting as distinguished from a single judge.

Bar Association: An association of members of the legal profession such as the California Bar Association (state level) and the American Bar Association (national level).

Bench: All judges taken collectively.

Blue Back: A blue paper sheet attached to the back and folded over the top edge of a pleading. The title of the pleading is abbreviated at the bottom of the blue back and the top is stamped either "original" for the original copy of the pleading, or "duplicate" if it is a copy. Many federal courts require pleadings to be "blue backed" before being submitted to them.

Calendar: (1) Court Calendar. A list of cases awaiting trial or other action. May include a listing of schedules, motions, or other pretrial matters. (2) In-House Calendar or Firm Calendar. An intra-office listing of important dates such as hearings, trials, court meetings, filing deadlines, scheduled depositions, etc., for use by attorneys and legal assistants in making all needed preparations for important events. An in-house calendar can be stored on a word processor or microcomputer and updated whenever a change occurs, thus providing users with an up-to-the-minute calendar of important future events at any given time.

Caption: The introductory page of a legal pleading that states the names of the attorneys, the parties to the action, file number of the action, title of the pleading, and the title of the court to which it is being submitted. (Sometimes called a Caption Page, Face Sheet or Cover Page.)

Cite (Citation of Authorities): The quoting of or reference to specific legal authorities and precedents to support one's legal position or refute the claims or positions of another. (See also Authority.)

Complaint: In civil law, the first pleading filed in a lawsuit which sets out the matters being complained of.

Company: An association of persons united to conduct some form of business enterprise.

Corporate: Belonging to or referring to a corporation.

Corporation: An entity created by or under the authority of the laws of a state or nation which has certain legal rights to exist and operate in the eyes of that legal system. There can be many different types of corporations, including business corporations, non-profit corporations, and professional corporations.

Declaration: A written statement in narrative form describing some event, or containing information of relevance to an ongoing legal case or other legal matter.

Defamation: A term which includes both libel and slander.

Defendant: The person or party who defends against a court action or lawsuit. The one against whom relief or remedy is being sought.

Demurrer: A pleading which objects to defects appearing on the face of a complaint or answer to complaint. A demurrer creates issues of law only and does not allege anything.

Deposition: (Generally) The oral questioning under oath of a witness or party to a lawsuit, outside of the courtroom, in order to obtain information of relevance to the case. A written transcript of the deposition is made and kept as a record of the deponent's testimony.

Discovery: The process of discovering facts relevant to a legal case which were not known previously. Through the process of "discovery," one party in a lawsuit may seek to discover what information or evidence relating to the dispute the opposing party has in its possession. Discovery may be accomplished in part by written questions (see interrogatories) or orally (see deposition).

Docket: A formal written record of the proceedings in a court of justice. The docket would contain a record in brief of each of the important events during the conduct of a particular case from beginning to end, including date and nature of any filed papers, orders, court appearances, and any verdicts rendered. Such a docket would be kept by the court clerk.

Exhibit: A document attached to an affidavit or pleading which gives evidence of some fact or has some relevance to the subject matter at hand, which when submitted to the court is then accepted as part of the case record. Exhibits can include charts, maps, affidavits, pleadings, or other relevant documents or things. Exhibits are usually numbered in sequence and immediately follow the pleading or affidavit in which they are referenced.

Ex Parte: Relating to, on behalf of, or submitted by only one party in a lawsuit or dispute. An "ex parte application," for example, is an application submitted for the benefit of one party and without notice to the other party.

Hearing: A formal meeting before a judicial body or court to decide on a particular motion or to hear evidence or to conduct some activity relevant to the case. A hearing is usually less formal and of shorter length than a trial. (See trial.)

Injunction: A writ or court order prohibiting a party from performing some action.

Interlocutory: The time period between the beginning of a lawsuit and the end of that lawsuit. Actions taken or decisions made during this time period which do not constitute a final decision to the whole case itself are said to be interlocutory.

Interrogatories: A question or set of questions directed in writing to a person or party who has knowledge of interest to a legal action. Interrogatories would usually be served as part of a discovery process. (Sometimes referred to informally as "interrogs" or "rogs." (See Discovery.)

Law: A body of rules of action or conduct prescribed by a controlling authority, such as a state or local government, and having binding legal force. There are many different types of law, such as civil law, criminal law, maritime law, administrative law, international law, and others.

Lawyer: A person licensed to practice law and whose business it is to give legal advice or assistance. (See also Attorney.)

Litigant: A party to a lawsuit.

Litigation: A contest in a court of law. A lawsuit.

Motion: An application made to a judge or court for the purpose of obtaining a ruling on a particular matter or requesting an order that some action be done or not done.

Memo of P's & A's (Memorandum of Points and Authorities):   A written document outlining specific points of legal argument and their supporting authorities. A memorandum of points and authorities would usually be filed as a supporting document to a particular motion or request for a court decision or action on some matter. (See also separately Point(s) and Authority.)

Minutes: The written record of proceedings at a meeting of the directors, officers or shareholders of a corporation.

Paralegal: An individual with legal training who works as part of a legal office or as an assistant to an attorney in the handling of legal matters. Some paralegals specialize in a particular area of law such as civil law, or criminal law. Paralegals are sometimes referred to as Legal Assistants.

PI (Preliminary Injunction):   A court order issued after a hearing which prohibits a party from performing a certain action or actions until a trial on the merits can be held.

Plaintiff: The person or party who brings a civil action or suit against another. The one who brings the complaint.

Pleadings: The formal written complaints or allegations of the parties involved in a dispute and their respective replies and defenses.

Point(s):   A specific question of law arising in a legal matter.

Proof of Service: A signed document which provides evidence to show that a given document has been served upon a particular party. The proof of service is signed by the one who serves the document. Proofs of service are required to follow certain formats depending on the court to which the proof is being submitted.

Retainer: (Generally) A specified sum of money requested by an attorney before he agrees to begin representation or start research on behalf of a particular client. A retainer may cover specific services or may be part of a general agreement under which an attorney agrees to make himself available for legal work as needed.

Service of Process: The service of summonses, writs, etc., to the person or party to whom they are directed. The one who delivers the document being served is often called the process server. Service can be effected in numerous different ways depending on the court requirements and related circumstances involved in the particular matter being handled.

Subpoena: A command by a court or legal authority to appear at a given time and place to give testimony on a particular matter.

SDT (Subpoena Duces Tecum): A command to appear and bring with one, certain specified documents, records or things. (See Subpoena.)

TOA (Table of Authorities): A listing in legal document of all the authorities relied upon in that document. A table of authorities may contain cases, statutes, court rules, and other authorities. (See Chapter 3 for an example of a table of authorities.)

TOC (Table of Contents): A listing of the contents in a legal document or pleading. A table of contents usually precedes a table of authorities in order of formatting a pleading. (See Chapter 3 for an example of a table of contents.)

Trial: A judicial examination and determination of issues between two or more parties to an action. A trial usually results in a final determination of issues.

TRO (Temporary Restraining Order): An emergency court order of brief duration which prohibits some action or activity until a further determination can be made.

Venue: A term describing the state, city or location in which a legal proceeding may be heard.

Verdict: The decision of a jury on the matters submitted to it for determination.

Verification: (1) A signed document attesting to the truth or correctness of some subject matter or evidence. (2) Oral confirmation of such truth or correctness.

Versus: (Latin) Against. Abbreviated "vs." or "v". Used in describing the relationship between parties in a lawsuit, such as *Jones vs. Smith* or *Harrison v. Jacobs.*

Will: A document on which a person sets out his wishes for the disposition of his property after his death.

Writ: An order issued from a court requiring the performance of some specified act or giving permission for a specific act to be done.

E   Abbreviations

acct.	account
a/p	accounts payable
agric.	agriculture
a.k.a.	also known as
amt.	amount
approx.	approximately
a/r	accounts receivable
a.s.a.p.	as soon as possible
assn.	association
asst.	assistant
avg.	average
bal.	balance
B/L	bill of lading
bldg.	building
B/S	bill of sale
chg.	charge
co.	company
c/o	care of
C.O.D.	cash on delivery
com.	commercial
comm.	commission
cont'd.	continued
corp.	corporation
cr.	credit

BUSINESS ABBREVIATIONS

dept.	department
disc.	discount
div.	division
dr	debit
dba	doing business as
ea.	each
encl.	enclosure
exp.	expense
f.o.b.	free on board
f.y.i.	for your information
ID	identification
Inc.	incorporated
ins.	insurance
int.	interest
invt.	inventory
ltd.	limited
max.	maximum
Messrs.	Misters
mfg.	manufacturing
mgmt.	management
mgr.	manager
min.	minimum
misc.	miscellaneous
mo.	month
n.	footnote
No.	number
Nos.	numbers
note	footnote
org.	organization
orig.	original
PABX	private automated branch exchange
pd.	paid
P & L	profit and loss
PO	purchase order
P.O.	post office
POS	point of sale
P.S.	post script
pres.	president
PR	public relations

recd.	received.
reg.	registered
req.	requisition
sec.	secretary
stmt.	statement
treas.	treasurer
TTY	teletype
V.P.	vice president

A.B.A.	American Bar Association	**LEGAL ABBREVIATIONS**
assn.	association	
ass'n	association	
attny.	attorney	
bus. & prof.	business & professions	
co.	company	
civ.	civil	
civ. proc.	civil procedure	
com.	commercial	
const.	constitution	
corp.	corporation	
cir.	circuit	
CCH	Commerce Clearing House	
Ct.	court	
Cf.	Latin: "compare"	
C.J.	chief justice, chief judge	
C.J.S.	Corpus Juris Secundum	
crim.	criminal	
d.b.a.	doing business as	
def.	defense	
depo.	deposition	
dep't	department	
et seq.	Latin: et sequentia, meaning "and the following"	
F.	Federal Reporter	
F.2d	Federal Reporter, Second Series	
Fed.	Federal	
F. Supp.	Federal Supplement	

id.	"idem" Latin, "the same"
Inc.	incorporated
I.R.C.	Internal Revenue Code
J.	judge
Juris Dr.	juris doctor
L.	law
law.	lawyer
ltd.	limited
n.	footnote
No.	number
Nos.	numbers
note	footnote
org.	organization
orig.	original
p.	page
pp.	pages
para.	paragraph
Pat. Pend.	patent pending
PI	private investigator
PI	preliminary injunction
TOA	table of authorities
TOC	table of contents
S. Ct.	Supreme Court
SDT	subpoena duces tecum
stat.	statute
U.S.C.	United States Code
U.S.C.A.	United States Code Annotated
vol.	volume

INFORMATION PROCESSING ABBREVIATIONS

ANSI	American National Standards Institute
AS	administrative support
ASCII	American Standard Code for Information Interchange
BAL	basic assembly language
BASIC	beginners all purpose symbolic instruction code
bit	binary digit
bps	bits per second

CAD	computer aided design
CAI	computer aided instruction
CBBS	computerized bulletin board system
CDP	certificate in data processing
CICS	customer information and control system
CMS	conversational monitoring system
COBOL	common business oriented language
COM	computer output on microfilm
CODASYL	conference on data system languages
cpi	characters per inch
cps	characters per second
CPU	central processing unit
CR	carriage control
CRT	cathode ray tube
CTRL	control
CTS	clear to send
CWP	communicating word processors
DASD	direct access storage device
DBMS	data base management system
DDP	distributed data processing
DOS	disk operating system
DMA	direct memory access
DP	data processing
DSK	Dvorak simplified keyboard
DTE	data terminal equipment
EBCDIC	extended binary coded decimal interchange code
EDP	electronic data processing
EFTS	electronic funds transfer system
EM	electronic mail
EOF	end of file
EOM	end of message
EOT	end of transmission
FIFO	first in, first out
FORTRAN	formula translation
GASP	gas plasma display
GIGO	garbage in, garbage out
IC	integrated circuit
I/O	input/output
IEO	integrated electronic office
IMS	information management system
IPL	initial program load
IPN	information processing network

K	kilobyte
Kb	kilobyte
LAN	local area network
LCD	liquid crystal display
LED	light emitting diode
LP	line printer
lpm	lines per minute
lps	lines per second
LSI	large scale integration
M	megabyte (1024 kilobytes)
Mb	megabyte (1024 kilobytes)
MIS	management information system
MSR	management support representative
MTST	magnetic tape selectric typewriter
NLQ	near letter quality
NRC	noise reduction coefficient
OA	office automation
OCR	optical character reader
OS	operating system
PABX	private automated branch exchange
PC	personal computer
RAM	random access memory
ROM	read only memory
RM	records management
R/W	read/write
SAM	sequential access method
SNA	system network architecture
SYSGEN	system generation
T/S	time sharing
TSO	time sharing option
TSS	time sharing system
TTY	teletypewriter
TWX	teletypewriter exchange service
VDT	video display terminal
VLSI	very large scale integration
VM	virtual memory
WP	word processing

†	dagger, death or deceased	**SYMBOLS**
§	section	
§§	sections	
¶	paragraph	
¶¶	paragraphs	
©	copyright	
™	trademark	
®	registered	
@	at	
$	dollar sign	
#	number	
%	percent	
*	asterisk	
&	ampersand, "and"	
<	less than	
>	greater than	
=	equals	
+	plus, positive	
−	minus, negative	

Alabama	AL	**U.S. STATES &**
Alaska	AK	**TERRITORIES**
Arizona	AZ	
Arkansas	AR	
California	CA	
Colorado	CO	
Connecticut	CT	
Delaware	DE	
District of Columbia	DC	
Florida	FL	
Georgia	GA	
Guam	GU	
Hawaii	HI	
Idaho	ID	
Illinois	IL	
Indiana	IN	
Iowa	IA	
Kansas	KS	
Kentucky	KY	
Louisiana	LA	

Maine	ME
Maryland	MD
Massachusetts	MA
Michigan	MI
Minnesota	MN
Mississippi	MS
Missouri	MO
Montana	MT
Nebraska	NE
Nevada	NV
New Hampshire	NH
New Jersey	NJ
New Mexico	NM
New York	NY
North Carolina	NC
North Dakota	ND
Ohio	OH
Oklahoma	OK
Oregon	OR
Pennsylvania	PA
Puerto Rico	PR
Rhode Island	RI
South Carolina	SC
South Dakota	SD
Tennessee	TN
Texas	TX
Utah	UT
Vermont	VT
Virgin Islands	VI
Virginia	VA
Washington	WA
West Virginia	WV
Wisconsin	WI
Wyoming	WY

Index